GREAT SPORTING MOMENTS

GOLF

The Last 25 Years

GREAT
SPORTING
MOMENTS

GOLF

The Last 25 Years

MIKE BRITTEN

WHSMITH
EXCLUSIVE
· BOOKS ·

SPORTS EDITIONS LIMITED

Managing Director	Richard Dewing
Creative Director	Mary Hamlyn
Art Director	Rob Kelland
Senior Designer	Sandra Cowell
Design Assistant	Lyndon Brooks
Editor	Tom Whiting

This edition published by W H Smith Ltd 1991

Produced in association with
Book Connections Limited
47 Norfolk Street
Cambridge CB1 2LE

ISBN 0 906782 54 6

Produced, edited and designed by
Sports Editions Limited
3 Greenlea Park
Prince George's Road
London
SW19 2JD

Typeset in Palatino and Frutiger by Sports Editions Limited
Origination by J. Film Process Co. Ltd, Bangkok
Printed by New Interlitho SpA, Milan

CONTENTS

INTRODUCTION

There is no limit to the ingenuity of man, especially when he applies it to pursuing the game of golf. From the Arctic to the Equator to the Antarctic there is hardly a country where the game is not being played, and it was the first of man's sporting pastimes to join the space age when astronaut Alan Shepherd interrupted his Moonwalk to strike golf balls from an imaginary lunar tee.

Well over a century earlier the colonising British, led enthusiastically by the Scots had begun taking the game to all corners of the globe, and the epidemic has gone on spreading like wildfire. Golf has shown it can transcend most barriers, and China and the Soviet Union have now joined the family of golf nations. Interest is also growing rapidly in those countries previously cocooned behind the Iron Curtain. Moscow recently opened its first 18-hole championship standard golf course constructed with turf grown in Finland, then shipped to the Russian capital on a convoy of lorries by a Swedish entrepreneur who was the first to realise that glasnost could be adapted to golf. There to maintain the tradition of the Caledonian golf pioneers, and strike the first celebratory ball was 007 himself, Sean Connery. Golf is also played by the blind, the armless and the legless, by male and female, young and old. It is thus of truly universal appeal, and fuelled by the growth of leisure in the late 20th century, is probably the fastest growing participation sport, with the number of players nearing 100 million. The great majority are amateurs, indulging a primaeval instinct to strike a stone with a stick, yet simultaneously benefiting from healthy exercise and friendly competition against like-minded companions.

Whether they are congregating among the Lapland reindeer at Bjorkliden, which claims to be the world's most northerly golf club, among the camels in the Arabian desert where the greens are "browns" of rolled sand mixed with oil, or with the penguins on makeshift holes laid out on the frozen wastes around Antarctic survey stations, they are united by their consuming love of golf. Amateurs are, of course, the life-blood of the game , which is governed by the Royal and Ancient Club of St Andrews and the United States Golf Association. This book is for, but not about, that play-for-fun majority. It concerns itself with those who were born with a special talent, chose to make golf their career, and have applied their gifts so successfully that they have become supreme champions. Goodness knows what those bewhiskered Victorians, who made their living from making hickory-shafted clubs and caddying for the aristocracy, would have made of today's jet-set professionals and their million-dollar prize funds. They would certainly be flabbergasted at how rapidly the gospel of the game has spread during the last 25 years. In that respect Messrs Palmer, Nicklaus and Player have been profoundly effective pioneers, adding great lustre to their profession, and continuing to do so in the autumn of their careers as architects and elder statesmen. They have made major contributions to the cause of making every country the home of golf, and others such as Ballesteros and Faldo will surely follow suit when their championship days are over.

Each generation owes a debt to the previous one. Future historians may have cause to disagree, but it is my belief that the era dominated by the Big Three of Arnie, Jack and Gary will be of much greater significance than that of the first Great Triumvirate of Braid, Vardon and Taylor in the 20 years before the Great War.

The legacy of the illustrious trio that sprang to prominence in the 1960s is a vast booming business whose popularity shows no sign of waning. It is an inheritance which must not be squandered.

As leisure time expands so will the demand for more places to play golf. For every member of a private club in 1990 there were twice as many who had nowhere to play on a regular basis. Britain needs another 700 courses by the end of the century just to keep pace with the increasing numbers being attracted to the game. Such is the extent of the challenge facing today's administrators. If they tackle it with half the determination the players in this book brought to solving their problems, then the boom, in Britain at least, will not peter out, and the World will be a better place for it. Golfers of the calibre of Norman, Strange, Langer, Lyle, Stewart, Woosnam and Olazabal are carrying on the tradition, and their success has gone a long way towards abolishing the concept that golf is an elitist sport. They have certainly become elite, but few of them came from privileged backgrounds as a glance at the formative years of Jacklin and Trevino will reveal. It has been my privilege to have witnessed and reported much of the finest golf played by those who feature in these pages. They have provided a host of golden memories, none more arresting than the Open swansong of the man who began it all. They stood in their grateful thousands at St Andrews in 1990 to pay their homage. He said he would not be back, but even so he will he never be forgotten. Thanks again, Arnold.

Brief History

In 1991 Golf will welcome its first World Championship, its four major professional circuits will collectively offer around £75 million prize money, and there will be at least one, and often three or four tournaments for 51 weeks, the sole exception being that in which Christmas falls. By the end of the year Europe will have overtaken Japan as the second most lucrative arena for the professional to ply his trade, with a 37-week circuit worth a staggering £20 million.

The United States tour, which runs from the first week in January to the middle of December, will have a treasure chest of around £29 million, and the balance will be made up by the increasing awards on the Asian and Australasian circuits. All this in a World supposedly in the grip of a deep recession! The growth of golf over the last 25 years is one of sport's great success stories and nowhere has the expansion been more startling than in Europe where the game that was once the preserve of the aristocracy is now expanding at breakneck pace. Three quarters of the PGA European Tour's programme will be staged on the mainland continent with 14 countries combining in a common European cause. Fuelled by the worldwide successes of its star players, golf has become the fastest growing game, spreading right down to the grassroots of nations like France, Spain, Germany, and even little Sweden where there are already more than 300,000 golfers in a population of eight million. It has taken 500 years since the discovery of the New World by Columbus for Europe's statesmen to bury their differences and take positive steps towards unity. Golf has achieved that European ideal in just 20 years. The seeds were sown in 1971 when Britain's Professional Golf Association, which had catered since its foundation in 1901 primarily for the needs of the club professional, somewhat grudgingly accepted that there was now a new breed of golfer, one who wanted to play tournaments as a career, rather than combine the two functions together.

Tony Jacklin was not the first of the new trailblazers but he was by far the most successful, having headed for the USA in 1968 and developed his game to the level necessary to become Britain's first Open champion since Max Faulkner 18 years earlier. When Jacklin won the US Open in 1970 to graduate to world-class status, Britain had a new sporting hero who was not only inspiring his fellow professionals but was also awakening the interest of a nation for whom golf was still a game for the professional classes, certainly as far as England was concerned. At that time there were little more than a dozen tournaments in Britain and Ireland, and prize money was barely £250,000. Yet the clamour from the new generation of professionals was so insistent that the PGA was forced to move with the times. The decision to appoint former Ryder Cup golfer John Jacobs, who had made a successful career as a teaching professional in Britain and the United States, to develop the tournament side was to have far reaching consequences. The groundwork that Director General Jacobs did over the next four years laid the solid foundations for today's booming European circuit which is now producing the most talented players in the game. In 1971 Jacobs had only one such ace, the magnetic Jacklin, whom he persuaded to base his operations "at home" rather than in the USA and elsewhere. Sponsors were increasingly looking towards leisure pursuits as a new vehicle for corporate advertising, and Jacobs saw sooner than most, that the combination of sponsor, star performer and television could be the catalyst for the growth of golf in Britain and Europe, which at that time could not begin to match the quality of the American scene. Even so, progress in those pioneering days was painfully slow and it took another seven years before prize money reached the important £1 million milestone. The tournament players had achieved their autonomy in 1975 and shortly afterwards Jacobs handed over to the new division's secretary Ken Schofield who became its Executive Director.

The players' decision to pin their banner to the "European" mast, and switch to Sunday finishes paved the way for television to commit itself to widespread coverage at a time when Seve Ballesteros, Nick Faldo, and Sandy Lyle were beginning to make their reputations in the wake of Jacklin. Sponsors began flocking to golf for all the obvious commercial reasons, and the boom began to gather pace, especially after Ballesteros became the first European golfer to win the US Masters in 1980. The previous year he had won the Open for the first time, and along with another Spaniard, Antonio Garrido, had provided the first European presence in the Ryder Cup match at the Greenbrier, West Virginia where the visiting team was captained appropriately by Jacobs.

Manuel Pinero and Jose Maria Canizares, soon to be World Cup winners, were adding to Spanish prestige, the emergence of Bernhard Langer provided Germany with its own golf hero, and in Britain players like Mark James, Howard Clark, Ken Brown and Sam Torrance were also approaching maturity. In 1984 when prize money was heading toward £4 million, the PGA European tour took another significant step which was to give further impetus. The establishment of a business arm under the leadership of George O'Grady provided the ideal vehicle for corporate sponsors who, with the growing strength of the Common Market, found they inevitably had a stake in the burgeoning European golf scene. Further Masters and Open victories by Ballesteros in 1983 and 1984 were followed by Langer's win at Augusta the next year, and the first British Open for 16 years by Sandy Lyle at Sandwich. That signalled the end of American domination, but what really confirmed it was the resounding European victory in the 1985 Ryder Cup contest at the Belfry where the PGA club headquarters had been established after the split with the Tournament division ten years earlier. Jacklin, who had done so much to get the Euro-circuit off the ground, was the inspirational captain of a triumph which was truly European. Four Spaniards, three Englishmen, three Scots, a German and a Welshman regained the trophy after a phenomenal gap of 28 years.

That victory was to provide a huge boost to European golf prestige that led to further significant progress both on and off the course. Sponsors old and new were encouraged to provide bigger and better incentives for the players, who responded with complementary achievements. Ian Woosnam and David Llewellyn won the World Cup for Wales in 1987, a year in which Woosnam won eight times around the world and took his winnings to over £1 million. Nick Faldo won his first Open title at Muirfield, and then led England to victory in the Dunhill Cup. Capping all that was another Ryder Cup triumph at Muirfield Village, Ohio where Jacklin's men inflicted on the USA its first home defeat since the match began in 1927.The quality of golf produced by the Europeans stunned American galleries who believed their side was invincible. They knew better after Jack Nicklaus saw his team "whitewashed" in the first series of fourballs. Europe now had its "Famous Five" — Ballesteros, Faldo, Langer, Lyle and Woosnam — and they went on to even greater heights. Lyle became the first

Briton to win the Masters in 1988, then Faldo took the Green Jacket in 1989 and 1990 in addition to being crowned Open champion for a second time. Both he and Woosnam nearly won the US Open in successive years, and the Five became the "Magnificent Seven" when Ireland's Ronan Rafferty took the European number one spot in 1989 and Spain's Jose Maria Olazabal flew into Akron and flew out with the 1990 World Series title, starting with a 61 at Firestone and ending with a 12-stroke victory over all the best Americans. Back home, sponsors continued to climb aboard the European bandwagon, which had gone into overdrive with the signing of a five-year sponsorship deal worth around £20 million with Volvo, the Swedish car manufacturer. Prize money leapt to £10 million in 1988, reached £13.5 million the following year, and in 1990 topped £16 million. Another quantum leap in 1991 took it through the psychological £20 million barrier to signify two decades of spectacular progress.

The advent of satellite television has brought golf from all corners of the globe into the living room, and when Europe retained the Ryder Cup, now sponsored on this side of the Atlantic by whisky giant Johnnie Walker, with the exciting 1989 tied match at the Belfry, the exploits of Seve and Co reached an audience of over 200 million. Numerous other business developments have followed in the wake of playing success, and having sparked the upsurge of interest in the game, the PGA European Tour is now at the forefront in helping to satisfy the huge public demand for places to play.

Europe is festooned with new golf projects and France alone will have doubled its stock of courses to over 400 by the end of this year. Somewhere out there are the new generation of aspiring champions, perhaps being inspired, as Lyle and Faldo were, by what they see on their television screens. They could be called Sandy or Nick, or maybe Pierre, Manuel, Franz or Guiseppe, but those who do pass through perhaps the toughest apprenticeship in any sport, will surely find fame, and certain fortune. Thanks to the pioneers, this truly is the Golden Age of Golf.

THE STARS

A phenomenon of modern professional golf has been the proliferation of accomplished players. In a high profile sport they have come to be labelled 'Superstars', an overworked but nevertheless appropriate term for those whose skill and artistry set them apart from the merely capable.

Millionaires to a man, they enjoy a lifestyle that is the envy of all who ever dreamed of winning an Open Championship or the US Masters, or sinking the decisive putt in the Ryder cup. Most are idolised, some inspire lifelong devotion, but all are definitely a breed apart.

Few will cavill at this selection of the top ten stars of the last 25 years, although I have been unable to find room for Australia's Peter Thomson or the great Argentinian Roberto de Vicenzo. Both were in the autumn of their careers in the mid-sixties.

Pride of place goes naturally to the man who has transcended all others in the history of the game. The 18 Major victories of Jack Nicklaus between 1962 and 1986 constitute a record that may never be eclipsed. The charisma of Palmer and Ballesteros, the indomitable spirit of Gary Player and the supreme skill of Watson and Trevino have at times prevailed, yet for a quarter of a century the Golden Bear has towered over them all. Tony Jacklin and Sandy Lyle gave Britain its first 'Superstars' and Nick Faldo is now the man everyone else, including Greg Norman and Payne Stewart (photo left), has to beat. Some of Faldo's fiercest rivals are among the 15 other luminaries in this chapter. The common factor is that each has already made an outstanding contribution to golf.

Isao Aoki

With his distinctive putting style and swing, Isao Aoki has spearheaded the Japanese challenge to the West's domination of the sport in the eighties.

Japan's best known golfer has not won a Major title but he was the first from the Far East to become a truly international golfer, and between 1978 and 1983 was high among the World's best.

Aoki, who was born in Abiko, Chiba on 31st August 1942, turned professional in 1964 but had to wait almost seven years for the first of more than 50 victories on his home circuit. It was not until 1978 that the rest of the golfing world got the chance to recognise his prowess when he formed the spearhead of a considerable Japanese contingent competing in the 1978 British Open at St Andrews. His heel-down, toe-up putting style was as distinctive as his 'flicky' swing, but both worked efficiently and took him into the halfway lead on his first outing on the Old Course. Aoki's linguistic talent was put to a severe test when he was duly summoned to describe his performance to the World media. When the R & A press officer continually pointed to the floor to emphasise his conviction that the Japanese had occasionally found trouble with the rough, both Aoki and his interpreter looked mystified. Isao the inscrutable then revealed further showmanship qualities by ultimately remarking in perfect English that he thought the carpet was of excellent quality.

He finished alongside the emerging Nick Faldo in seventh place behind Jack Nicklaus,

Intense concentration is a hallmark of Isao Aoki's game (above) and at the 1986 US Masters he used this to great effect (right) in escaping the bunkers. In his early career, he came within a whisker of beating Jack Nicklaus at the 1980 US Open (far right)

with whom he had an epic duel for the US Open at Baltusrol, New Jersey in 1980. But first Aoki made himself a household name by winning the World Matchplay championship at Wentworth in the autumn of 1978, and the following season acquired a British house with the shot of the year. He produced it at the second hole of his second round match with Australian David Graham. Aoki struck a 7-iron shot across the valley to the elevated green which pitched a foot from the hole and jumped straight in.

The 1983 European Open Champion, and looking well pleased!

Aoki's ace won him a fully furnished home at Gleneagles before most of his rivals had finished their breakfast. The developers who had donated the award had wisely insured against a hole-in-one by placing a £1,000 bet with a London bookmaker at odds of 40-1.

Aoki went on to outlast Seve Ballesteros in a semi-final that went to four extra holes before falling to a last green birdie from Bill Rogers in the final. The Japanese journeyman had shown a remarkable capacity for endurance that was to serve him well during his finest year at the age of 37.

He played with Nicklaus throughout that 1980 US Open and had three consecutive rounds of 68 to share the lead with the Golden Bear who had opened with a 63. Their 54-hole totals of 204 were a new record. Their fourth outing was virtual matchplay with Aoki refusing to surrender to an opponent playing flawlessly. The outcome was in doubt to the very end of a thrilling contest. Baltusrol ends with two par fives, measuring 630 and 542 yards. Aoki birdied both, but so did Nicklaus to win his fourth US Open by two strokes with a 68 to Aoki's 70. Their totals of 272 and 274 have not yet been surpassed. A month later the Japanese shot 63 in the British Open at Muirfield to equal the low round record.

Back home he achieved the God-like status enjoyed by great rival Jumbo Ozaki, especially after becoming the first from Japan to win on the US Tour when he took the 1983 Hawaiian Open. Playing the last, he needed a birdie to win, but Aoki, with his gift for the spectacular, made doubly sure. He sank a 130 yards pitch from the rough for an eagle 2. He was soon back in Britain, winning the European Open at Sunningdale that autumn.

CAREER HIGHLIGHTS

Major titles
Nil

Worldwide victories 57
including
World Match Play: 1978
European Open: 1983
Hawaiian Open: 1983
Dunhill Cup: 1985
Japan v USA: 1982-83-84

Seve Ballesteros

The farmer's son from Santander in Spain burst upon the Championship scene in 1976 and has since dazzled the world with his flamboyant genius and charismatic style.

Only time will decide whether Seve Ballesteros will rank among the immortals of golf. Three British Opens and two US Masters have certainly brought him into serious consideration and he was unquestionably the outstanding golfer of the 1980s —which he ended with 60 worldwide victories to his credit. Yet he has still not captured a US Open or US PGA Championship so the jury must remain out. He has perhaps another seven years in which to achieve those goals, but if he never again enjoys such a significant success Ballesteros will always be lauded as the inspiration of European golf.

From the moment he burst upon the Championship scene in the 1976 Open at Royal Birkdale, the dashing genius from Santander became the trail-blazer for all those striving to end the years of American domination of the game's major honours. Within three years he was Open champion, and when the rank and file US tour professionals disparagingly dubbed him a 'car park champion' he slapped them down with a commanding 1980 Masters victory. Seve has gone on punishing them ever since, taking special delight in the European Ryder Cup victories of 1985 and 1987, the latter providing him with the stage to display some of the finest golf of his career.

Almost single-handedly he has raised the standard of British and European golf to today's level, impressing on others that the Americans could be beaten. Germany's Bernhard Langer was the first to follow suit, then Sandy Lyle and Nick Faldo conquered the citadel of Augusta. Ian Woosnam and

A fine shot! Seve inspires the Europeans in the 1985 Ryder Cup

Jose Maria Olazabal have also made their mark in the USA in the wake of Ballesteros.

Like Trevino and before him Hogan, Seve, who was born on 9th April 1957, came into golf via the caddy ranks. Youngest of four brothers — all golf professionals — he learnt to play with a cut-down 3-iron given to him by brother Manuel. The Pedrena course was only a stone's throw from the house where father Baldomero 'farmed' a smallholding with a few animals.

Seve would sneak on to the course before the members arrived, and at dusk after they had left, to play with his 3-iron. He learnt to execute every shot in the bag, including bunker recoveries, with that club. At 14 he was caddies champion and just after his 16th birthday he became the youngest ever to be granted professional status by the Spanish Golf Federation. In 1974, when just 17, he was runner-up for the Italian Open — a tournament his uncle, Ramon Sota, had won three years previously.

In those early days Ballesteros hit the ball

everywhere, finding parts of the course other players could not reach. Then he extricated himself from trouble with a bewildering variety of escape shots. It was exhilarating and exhausting for the galleries, but they never tired of the excitement.

After two cavalier opening rounds of 69 on his Open debut at Birkdale, he led the field and the world knew a new star was born. The experience of Johnny Miller prevailed, but Ballesteros tied second with Nicklaus, went on to win the Dutch Open

Taking time off to face the Press at the 1986 US Masters (above) and two years later at the same event, agonisingly close at the 10th (left) as brother Vincente remonstrates with the ball

and Lancome Trophy and finished the year as European Number One at the age of 19.

By Lytham 1979 he was ready for his first Major, although his driving was still erratic. But he more than made up for it with his recovery powers and superb short game. His pitching, bunker play and putting were a class apart. A second round 65 laid the foundation of a three-stroke win over Nicklaus and Ben Crenshaw.

Seve scored a second Masters win in 1983 and the following year took his second Open

Not quite siesta time yet, just Ballesteros and Olazabal experiencing a nightmarish moment at the Ryder cup in 1989

at St Andrews after a thrilling duel with Tom Watson. His strategy of hitting left throughout to avoid the Old Course bunkers paid off, for three of his four rounds were under 70. Ultimately the title lay between the Spaniard and the American who was attempting to equal Vardon's record of six Open wins. Watson's mistake in over-clubbing to the Road Hole in the last round is perceived as the decisive moment of their contest. Ballesteros prefers to remember the 6- iron stroke he hit from the left rough at that hole to find the kidney-shaped green, and clinch the par four that Watson, unfortunately for him, could not match.

Seve had to wait until the Open returned to Lytham in 1988 to secure that fifth Major, although he was third in the US Open the previous year, his best finish there in a dozen attempts. In 1986 he had seen a third Masters torn from his grasp by Nicklaus, and the next year three-putted the first hole of the play-off in which Larry Mize chipped in to beat Greg Norman.

The return to the scene of first glory inspired the Spaniard, who produced a last round 65 to break clear of defending champion Nick Faldo, and Sandy Lyle, and overhaul third-round leader Nick Price. The title clinching stroke, a beautifully weighted chip from the side of the last green which brushed the hole was vintage Ballesteros.

A classic swing coupled with the imagination to conjure shots others could not even conceive has made Ballesteros by general acclaim the best player in the game. However, it is becoming harder than ever to win Majors and maybe the days are gone when one man could dominate his contemporaries in the manner of Hagen, Cotton, Hogan or Nicklaus. For the time being Ballesteros is simply 'El Magnifico'.

CAREER HIGHLIGHTS

Major titles

British Open: 1979-84-88

US Masters: 1980-83

Other achievements

Ryder Cup: 1979-83-85-87-89

World Cup: 1975-76-77

Leading money-winner in Europe: 1976-77-78-86-88 (first player to win £1 million prize money in Europe)

World Matchplay: 1981-82-84-85

Bob Charles

New Zealand-born Bob Charles graduated from bank clerk to golfing star; he remains the only left-hander to have captured a Major championship and has not looked back since that memorable day.

One of the mysteries of golf is why so few left-handers have become champions. Yorkshire's Peter Dawson remains the only one to have played in the Ryder Cup, appearing in the 1977 match at Royal Lytham when he beat Don January in his singles match. Yet the 'lefties' in golf suffer badly in comparison with their cricketing and tennis-playing kin. Gary Sobers, Neil Harvey, Alan Border and David Gower are just a few of those who have flourished in Test cricket, while Rod Laver, Tony Roche, John McEnroe and Martina Navratilova spring easily to mind from the roll of tennis champions. Bob Charles is golf's shining exception and remains the only left-hander to have captured one of the World's four Major Championships, in his case the 1963 British Open Championship. He was also second in 1968 and 1969 and was runner up for the 1968 US PGA title.

Robert James Charles was born in Carterton, New Zealand on 14th March 1936 and first made his mark when, still an amateur, he won the New Zealand Open in 1954 at the age of 18 years and 7 months. He led after every round and among the professionals he defeated was the then newly crowned British Open champion Peter Thomson.

Instead of rushing into the professional ranks the lean and lanky Charles refused to give up his job as a bank clerk until he was certain he could make a good living from

'Watch... it's all in the shoulders.' Bob Charles displays the unique art of being a left-handed golfer

golf. Not until after he had played for New Zealand in the 1960 World Amateur Championship did the lanky Kiwi make the switch and seek his fortune in Europe. So good was his putting stroke that success came quickly in the 1961 Bowmaker tournament, and the next year he won the Daks event and Swiss Open. Charles's accurate driving and iron play were impressive, but it was his unerring skill on the greens that made him a trend-setter. His stiff-wristed style and use of the shoulder rather than the wrists as the putting hinge, had many imitators and is the method most

On the way to becoming the first and only left-handed winner of the British Open at Royal Lytham and St Annes in 1963

Toying with sandcastles at the 1990 Open?

widely used around the golf circuits today, both at the amateur and professional levels.

Charles first won in the USA in 1963 but his greatest achievement came at Royal Lytham that summer when he tied with American Phil Rodgers and then beat him in the 36-hole play-off. Although Charles remained a regular migrant to Europe until 1985 he subsequently concentrated his efforts on the US circuit, and by 1974 had won five times there.

His other notable British triumphs came in the 1969 World Matchplay at Wentworth — where he beat Gene Littler at the 37th after sinking a 25 footer on the last green to take the final into extra-time — and the 1972 John Player Classic at the gale-swept Turnberry course.

Charles took to wearing spectacles for the first time in 1984, but still found the odds stacked against left-handers. A typical example occured during the European Open at Sunningdale when he was penalised two shots after his first round for moving a tee marker at the second because he found that it was impeding his backswing. 'It was no problem to a right-hander, but I guess they forgot about me,' he remarked with a wry smile, and this despite his disappointment.

Nowadays Charles is ensuring he will be remembered by his exploits on the US Seniors tour. Winner of the British Seniors Open when he returned to Turnberry in 1989, he had five American Senior wins that season to head the money list with a stroke average of 69.78. In 1990 he was a double winner and with that marvellous putting stroke still working smoothly had taken his Senior career winnings in the USA to an impressive $2.3 million.

CAREER HIGHLIGHTS

Major titles
British Open: 1963

Worldwide victories 54

Other achievements
World Cup: 1962-63-64-65-66-67-68-71-72
Dunhill Cup: 1985-86
World Amateur Champ: 1960

Ben Crenshaw

He was dubbed 'Gentle Ben' by his fellow professionals, but a competitive spirit allied to thoroughbred putting skills ensured that Ben Crenshaw would be no pushover when it came to a fight to the line.

Most professionals have a deep and lasting affection for the game, but none has conducted such a long-running love affair as Ben Crenshaw. The blond Texan is an avid collector of golf artefacts and memorabilia and his pride in his valuable hoard will provide some compensation for so many near misses in Major championships long after his tournament career is over.

Ben Daniel Crenshaw, born in Austin on 11th January 1952, has been one of the most popular professionals since he joined their ranks in 1973 following a distinguished amateur career. His knack of inspiring affection from fans and rivals alike has made him one of the best ambassadors for the game and he is held in as high esteem in the British Isles as he is in his home state.

His love of links golf and its rich history, coupled with his mellow personality, have earned him the soubriquet 'Gentle Ben', but Crenshaw's competitive edge has been as hard as any of his generation. He is renowned as one of the finest putters the game has ever seen, and proof of that came during his 1987 Ryder Cup singles against Eamonn Darcy at Muirfield Village. In a rare

Extracting himself from a spot of bother at the 1986 US Masters

The master craftsman, Ben has always been renowned for his fine putting, but here he shows he can drive with the best... how's that for a perfect follow-through!

fit of pique he broke his putter shaft early in that match, but got back on level terms by holing out on the greens, first with a sand wedge then his one-iron. It was not his putting failures that let in the Irishman to take his place in Ryder Cup history, but the Texan's propensity for ambitious yet destructive shots with his driver.

'Gentle Ben' nevertheless displays a competitive edge as great as any golfer of his generation

All through his career Crenshaw's wildness from the tee at key moments has cost him titles his otherwise immaculate golf has deserved. It is the main reason he had to

wait until 1984 for his first Major, the US Masters. In 1975 he should have been in the play-off for the US Open won by Lou Graham, but fired his tee shot at the penultimate hole into water. A double bogey at the 71st at Royal Lytham in 1979 handed the British Open to Seve Ballesteros and the same year he was on the brink of taking the US PGA title at Oakland Hills. He lost at the third hole of a sudden death play-off to Australian David Graham.

For a player who had been National Collegiate champion for three successive years prior to turning professional and had then won his first tournament, the Texas Open, those could have been mortal blows. Even his three US tour victories in 1976 and success in the Irish Open that year at Portmarnock were scant compensation.

Crenshaw finally bagged that overdue first Major at Augusta after waiting 11 years. To get there he had to beat Tom Watson, Tom Kite and Larry Nelson after starting with an immaculate 67. Two shots behind Kite at the start of the last day he enjoyed that stroke of luck which all champions need when he holed a roller coaster putt of some 25 yards for a birdie at the 10th when three putts were staring him in the face. A two at the short 12th put him in command, and although Watson kept charging to the end, Crenshaw held on for a 68 to gain the victory he described as a 'sweet, sweet thing'.

Such delights were unobtainable the following year, principally because of ill health in the form of an overactive thyroid. Yet he won twice in 1986 to clinch his third Ryder Cup appearance and stayed in the American top ten in 1987 and 1988, winning the World Cup and the Individual trophy in Melbourne. In 1990 he gained his 15th tour win and remains a consistent money winner.

CAREER HIGHLIGHTS

Major titles
US Masters: 1984

US Tour victories 15

Other achievements
Ryder Cup: 1981-83-87
World Cup: 1972, 1988

Nick Faldo

'Mr Consistency' has combined natural talent with a cast-iron concentration and a will to succeed, to become one of the most successful golfers to have graced the game. He remains a role model to all budding golf enthusiasts.

Perfection is an impossible goal for any sportsman but Nick Faldo has come closest to achieving 100 per cent rating in the last four years. A combination of natural talent, hard work and strong nerve has taken the elegant Englishman to the superstar stratosphere, to the level where he has become the benchmark by which others judge success.

Open champion for the first time in 1987, when he produced a final round of 18 pars, perfectionist Faldo soared to world beater in 1990 when he won the Masters for the second successive year, came within a whisker of taking the US Open for which he had tied in 1988, then strode unopposed to a second Open triumph at St Andrews. It was the nearest anyone had come to emulating Hogan's 1953 treble of the two Opens and the Masters, and provoked much speculation of his future chances of the modern Grand Slam. Faldo was 'only' 18th in the 1990 US PGA at Shoal Creek Alabama to underline the near impossibility of a Major clean sweep.

For the moment the remorseless manner in which he destroys a Championship course and the spirit of his rivals makes Faldo the

'Hmm, not an Aussie in sight...'

Springtime at Augusta sees Nick blazing away (right), and in a contrasting sombre mood at the 1988 Open (far right)

best qualified to entertain hopes of gaining golf's Holy Grail. He has the most reliable swing in the modern game coupled with the ability to perform at his best under the most intense pressure. Both his Masters wins came after he prevailed in play-offs, further proof that he is the man for the big occasion.

Only Nicklaus had previously retained a Masters title, so when, in 1990, Faldo overcame Raymond Floyd at the very hole he had accounted for Scott Hoch the previous season, he could truly claim that it seemed like destiny. For Faldo, born on July 18th 1957 in Welwyn Garden City, might never have taken up the game had he not seen Jack Nicklaus on television, playing in the 1971 Masters. The 13-year-old Faldo was so smitten that the next day he persuaded his parents to book him a course of lessons at the local club.

Faldo found the challenges that golf makes to mind and body more suited to his temperament than traditional team games like football and cricket. He also excelled at cycling and was an above average swimmer, and his natural athleticism enabled him to quickly master the fundamentals of the game. Within three years he had graduated from novice to England Boy International and the summer of 1975 saw the first blossoming of an extraordinary talent. Along with Sandy Lyle he had come under the auspices of the Golf Foundation and when both entered senior competition at the same

time their impact was sensational.

Faldo won the Berkshire Trophy, the English Amateur Championship at Lytham, and the British Youths at Pannal near Harrogate, shortly after his 18th birthday. Clearly he was ready for a professional career. In 1977 he made his Ryder Cup debut before he had won a 72-hole tournament, returning to Lytham to beat Tom Watson in his singles, and linking with Peter Oosterhuis to defeat Nicklaus and Floyd in foursomes. The first of four European PGA victories arrived at Birkdale in 1978 and he became a prolific winner, taking five titles in 1983 to be European Number One. Faldo then captured the Sea Pines Heritage Classic in 1984 to show that he could be a multiple winner on the US tour.

However he knew his game lacked the consistency for him to become a Major winner, so he took the decision to reconstruct his swing, and turned to David Leadbetter, the British born coach who runs a teaching school in Florida. For two years Faldo concentrated on mastering the mechanics, 'retraining' his golf muscles, and perfecting a method on which he could rely.

The new Faldo formula first proved a success at Muirfield in 1987 when he held off

Paul Azinger with that celebrated parade of pars. Nowadays Faldo's workload on the practice ground and the constant fine-tuning required to keep his game in perfect pitch would buckle men of lesser determination, but his industry has made him a multi-millionaire with the potential to widen his interests to golf architecture and teaching.

There has, however, been a price to pay. 'Workaholic' Faldo unwittingly put his career in jeopardy in his pursuit of perfection by hitting too many balls on the practice range. Sore wrists curtailed his activities in the autumn of 1990 when expert examination revealed that he had created an imbalance of strength between the inner and outer arm muscles. His wrists could not cope with the continual strain he was imposing on them. Lasting damage was prevented by treatment and remedial exercises and Faldo is now poised to be the dominant golfer of the new decade. Nicklaus

Nick heads for glory at the Open in 1990 ...and Number One in the World rankings

declared on the eve of the 1990 Open that the status of World Number One was there to be claimed. The one who most believed in himself and could handle the fact that everyone else was shooting at him would reach the summit.

Faldo played the World's best golf throughout the year and when he destroyed the Open challenge of Greg Norman, the leader in the statistical rankings, Nicklaus and everyone else knew that a new King had taken his throne. The Englishman's greatness will now be measured by how long he can reign.

CAREER HIGHLIGHTS

Major titles

Four British Opens: 1987-90

US Masters: 1989-90

Other achievements

Ryder Cup: 1977-79-81-83-85-87-89

World Cup 1977

Leading money-winner in Europe: 1983

World Matchplay: 1989

Raymond Floyd

A taste for the good life would not prevent Ray Floyd from becoming one of the most respected journeymen around the golfing circuit.

For many years Ray Floyd's strongest claim to fame was that he managed the first topless all-girl dance band. By the time he captained the 1989 US Ryder cup team that gained a tie with Europe at the Belfry, he had become one of the most respected figures in American golf during a highly successful career spanning almost 30 years.

The tournament career of Raymond Loran Floyd began in 1963 , and initially was a long way from being the success he envisaged. Born on 4th September 1942 in Fort Bragg, North Carolina, where his father was stationed in the Army, Floyd failed to get beyond the halfway stage in his first ten tournaments. He then won the 11th, the St Petersburg Open, the first of his 21 US tour victories. It was another six years before Floyd, whose sister Marlene plays on the LPGA circuit, shook off his playboy image long enough to capture the first of his four Majors, the US PGA Championship at Dayton, Ohio. He also won twice more in 196, and this resulted in a move into the American top ten.

His flamboyant lifestyle continued to make more headlines than his shot-making ability until marriage and the birth of Raymond Junior in 1974 saw him settle down to acquire a more conventional popularity. Floyd won only once in 1975, but then produced a masterly performance to run away with the 1976 Masters. He employed one of the newly fashionable Zebra putters to gain more consistency on the greens, and tossed the one-iron out of his golf bag in favour of a five-wood. Floyd

At the advanced age of 48, and still going strong at the 1989 US PGA tournament

reasoned that the only way to hold the speedy greens at the long holes was to hit high second shots.

The five-wood gave him strategic air command and his eight-stroke victory was founded on his demolition of the par fives for which he was 13 under par. He opened with a 65, followed with a 66 and his 131 halfway total was a Masters record. So was his 54 hole score after a third round 70, and he closed with another 70 to equal the record aggregate of 271 set by the great Jack Nicklaus way back in 1965.

No buggy-bashers at the Belfry in 1989, just the adoring Stars and Stripes brigade (above), and weighing up a tricky putt (right)

One more for the trophy cabinet. Ray and family proudly display the 1986 US Open Championship trophy to the crowds at Shinnecock Hills

That performance made him one of the game's major figures and provided the springboard for quite remarkable success in middle age. In 1981 he had three further victories and the following year took his second US PGA title. Floyd's opening 63 at Tulsa's Southern Hills club ranks in his estimation as 'the best round of golf I have ever played anywhere in my life.' It also enabled him to enhance his reputation as one of the best front-runners as he set new marks for 36 and 54 holes and won by three shots over the field.

Floyd has always been an astute tactician with a highly effective, if sometimes ungainly, swing, and both facets of his game were at their most efficient at Shinnecock Hills for the US Open in 1986. Competing for the 22nd time Floyd had opened with a 75. However, he played the last three rounds in 204 strokes, and brilliantly seized his victory chance when it came over the last nine holes. He played them in 32 for a stunning 66, showing ice-cool nerve and solid technique in the severest test of emotional tension that he had ever been through.

At 43 years and nine months he was the oldest winner of the title until Hale Irwin claimed that honour at Medinah in 1990. Only the lack of a British Open prevents him joining the select group who have achieved the full set. Floyd came closest in 1978 when a closing 68 at St Andrews saw him tie second with Ben Crenshaw two shots behind Nicklaus. That was another example of the flair for the spectacular that has served the man from North Carolina so well in the past, and may continue to do so in the future.

CAREER HIGHLIGHTS

Major titles

US Open: 1986

US Masters: 1976

US PGA: 1969, 1982

US Tour victories 21

Others achievements

Ryder Cup: 1969-75-77-81-83-85

Captain 1989 US team

DAVID GRAHAM

As the first Australian to win the US Open back in 1981 on the tricky greens of Merion, Pennsylvania, the self-taught David Graham made his mark and established his credentials as a world class golfer.

Driving crisply through the ball on the 9th tee at a resplendent Turnberry ...

Bob Charles might have had a serious rival as the world's best left-hander had Australia's David Graham continued as he began the game. As a 14-year old Graham started playing golf with a set of left-handed clubs he discovered at home in up-country New South Wales. He used them for two years before switching to playing right-handed , then left home at 16, against his father's wishes, to work in a golf shop in Melbourne. After a spell as a club professional in Tasmania, Anthony David Graham, who was born in Windsor, NSW on 23rd May 1946, set out to conquer the World, initially heading for Europe in the footsteps of his great friend Bruce Devlin who had also turned professional early in 1962.

The largely self-taught Graham did not taste success until 1970 when he won the Victorian and Tasmanian Opens, and also won in Thailand. His first European victory came in the French Open at Chantaco near Biarritz in the same year. Those performances earned Graham his debut in the World Cup in Buenos Aires in

November, and he and Devlin took the trophy back to Australia for the first time since Peter Thomson and Kel Nagle's second success in 1959. Graham was just pipped for the individual trophy by the great Argentinian Roberto de Vicenzo, but at 24 he was on top of the world.

The US tour beckoned and after qualifying at the 1971 School, Graham quickly scored his first win there, taking the 1972 Cleveland Open. Further victories back home in Australia and in Japan established him as a world-class golfer, and four wins in 1976 when he journeyed to Europe to become World Matchplay champion, ending Hale Irwin's attempt at a Wentworth hat-trick, signalled he was ready to become a force in the Majors. Graham's glory arrived at Oakland Hills in Michigan when he became only the second overseas player to take the US PGA Championship. Gary Player had already won it twice but Graham's 1979 triumph was remarkable in that he too had to be doubly good.

... and finding escape from the bunkers at Augusta a rather tricky proposition

Four wins in 1976, culminating in the World Matchplay title, established David as a world-class performer

His opening rounds of 69-68-70 had put him four shots behind leader Rex Caldwell with Ben Crenshaw two ahead, but the Australian's immaculate strokeplay and inspired last-day putting sent him two shots clear on the final tee. He needed a par four for a 63, but the Australian let his thoughts race ahead, and hit a woeful tee shot into the gallery. His next went through the green and then he duffed his first chip. He took three more to get down and the double bogey meant a play-off with Crenshaw. Graham holed from 25 and 15 feet to share the first two extra holes, then won at the third with an eight foot birdie putt.

Two years later there was not the slightest trace of fortune when he became the first Australian to win the US Open at Merion, Pennsylvania. Tight fairways and small, speedy greens make Merion one of America's most difficult trials, but Graham played it to near perfection in a final round of 67 that contained 33 putts to win by a stroke. His best British Open finish remains a third place behind Sandy Lyle at Sandwich in 1985, but he was a winner again in Britain the following year when he joined up with Greg Norman and Rodger Davis to secure the cherished Dunhill Cup for a jubilant Australia at St Andrews.

CAREER HIGHLIGHTS

Major titles

US Open: 1981

US PGA: 1979

US Tour victories 8

Other achievements

World Cup: 1970 (winner with Bruce Devlin)

Dunhill Cup: 1985-86-88

Hale Irwin

Just when it was thought that the studied American had shot his bolt, Hale Irwin battled against the odds to triumph gloriously in the 1979 US Open at the grand age of 45, and five years after his first success.

High fives, the in-vogue recognition for feats of sporting excellence, are not the gestures one expects from Hale Irwin. With his avuncular air, the once bespectacled American looks more like a schoolmaster or bank manager than an over-emotional golf hero. Yet everyone understood his exuberance when he holed a 45-foot last green birdie putt to earn a play-off place in the 1990 US Open, and then went on to win the title for a third time after another 19 holes of head-to-head conflict with fellow American Mike Donald.

Irwin, champion in 1974 and 1979, created history at Chicago's Medinah club when, at the age of 45, he replaced Raymond Floyd as the oldest winner of the US title. Scampering around that last green, slapping hands with everyone within reach, was Hale's version of a lap of honour he richly deserved, even if it looked completely out of character. As comebacks go it was mightily impressive considering he had not won on the US circuit since the Memorial Tournament in 1985. But then the man from Joplin, Missouri has always been a force on courses requiring precision golf.

The first of Irwin's US Opens was gained at New York's Winged Foot where ten of the dozen par fours measure over 400 yards. The second came at Inverness in Toledo, Ohio where the premium is also on long, accurate second shots. Irwin's well controlled strokeplay, coupled with consistency and a competitive heart, also brought him success in Europe, particularly during the 1970s when he twice won the World Matchplay

'Fancy a plumb line?' Hale perhaps recalling that crucial two inch putt he missed in the 1983 Open

'Hale-bent' on finding the green at St Andrews

title at Wentworth, and was denied a hat-trick in 1976 only by a barrage of miraculous putts from Australian David Graham.

A marketing graduate from the University of Colorado, Irwin turned professional in 1968 and enjoyed the first of his 19 US Tour wins in 1971. Throughout the decade he was a major figure on both sides of the Atlantic, and also won in South Africa, Australia and Japan. In seven years he was never less than seventh on the US Money list and between 1975 and 1978 did not miss a cut in 86 tournaments — a remarkable feat.

Hale has won on most of the best American courses, including Riviera, Pinehurst No 2 and Pebble Beach — the latter in 1984 providing him with his most unusual victory. Needing a birdie at the 18th to tie with Canadian Jim Nelson, he pulled his drive on to the beach of Carmel Bay. His ball struck a rock, rebounded on to the fairway, and Irwin got his birdie, going on to take the play-off.

Nelson took that setback philosophically, which is more than Irwin had done when he was forced to witness Seve Ballesteros' powers of escapology in winning the 1979 Open at Royal Lytham. The Spaniard missed most of the fairways in the final round which Irwin began with a two-shot lead, but was then dismissed as a 'car park champion' by the US Open title holder who seemed to have temporarily forgotten his own double bogey-bogey finish a month earlier at Inverness up in Scotland.

Irwin fell away to a 78 to finish five strokes behind, and then squandered his next chance of a British Open title at Royal Birkdale in 1983 by having an air shot with his putter, missing the tiniest of 'tiddlers'. He finished joint second, one behind Tom Watson. A rejuvenated Irwin is now eagerly awaiting a return to the US Ryder Cup team against Europe at Kiawah Island, South Carolina in the autumn of 1991.

A victory jig for Hale Irwin in the 1990 US Open at Medinah

CAREER HIGHLIGHTS

Major titles

US Open: 1974-79-90

US Tour victories 19

Other achievements

Ryder Cup: 1975-77-79-81

World Cup: 1974-79 (Individual winner 1979)

Tony Jacklin

From becoming the first British Open winner for 18 years, through to an OBE award and captaining a triumphant European Ryder Cup crusade, Tony Jacklin has been through the lot.

The name of Tony Jacklin is now inextricably linked with European Ryder Cup success. As captain of the team that won back the trophy at the Belfry in 1985, inflicted the first home defeat on the USA at Muirfield Village two years later, and then retained the Cup with a tie in 1989, Jacklin is assured of an honoured place in the history of the game.

Those who were present at either of the first two occasions, will freely testify to the massive contribution he made to events that provided the year's great sporting moments. Jacklin himself described that mid-September afternoon in 1985 when a tearful Sam Torrance beat Andy North to bring the trophy home for the first time in 28 years as 'the day European golf came of age'.

Europe's 1987 victory on the course that Jack Nicklaus built in Ohio was in Jacklin's words a dream come true. 'The satisfaction I gained from that was immense,' he said. 'It was the best week of my golfing career.' That had begun when the lorry driver's son from Scunthorpe who was born on 7th July 1944, quit work as an apprentice in the local steelworks and managed to find work as an assistant at the famous Potters Bar club on the outskirts of North London.

His boss was former Australian Rugby

Determination etched on his face as Jacklin chips out from one of the many Royal Lytham bunkers during the 1988 Open

Youthful exuberance pays off as Jacklin triumphs at the 1969 Open in front of a partisan crowd

League player Bill Shankland. Jacklin found him a hard taskmaster and soon made it clear that he wanted more out of golf than selling tee pegs and giving lessons to club members. The latter raised the cash to send him to the 1963 Open at Royal Lytham where the 19-year-old Jacklin finished 30th behind New Zealand left-hander Bob Charles. Six years later Tony returned in triumph to the Lancashire links and first became the darling of the nation by becoming the first British golfer to win the Open since Max Faulkner in 1951. Yet already he had signalled his ambition to reach the top and he made the most of his good fortune when he got an unexpected invitation to the 1967 US Masters. Augusta inspired Jacklin. He qualified easily for the final 36 holes, led the field at one stage during the third round, and went on to finish a creditable 16th.

A first British victory soon followed, then he scored a spectacular Dunlop Masters success at Royal St George's, taking away

Cotton's 33-year-old course record with a last round 64. Jacklin joined the US tour in 1968 and within eight weeks had become the first Briton to win there since Ray's US Open in 1920. His win at Jacksonville, which he repeated in 1972, encouraged Tony to enigmatically declare that he wanted to win all the Major championships of the world and become a millionaire.

Shortly after his 25th birthday he took the first step on the road to both goals. Jacklin satisfied the sporting needs of a nation starved of golf success when he started the last round of the 1969 Open with a two-shot lead over Charles, and never lost it. His final drive was propelled with such power and accuracy that there was never a doubt that he would give British golf the shot in the arm it so desperately needed. The crowd broke into an emotional rendering of 'For he's a Jolly Good Fellow' and there was hardly a dry eye on the links. Later that summer Jacklin was again the hero when his half with Nicklaus in the final singles earned

Thrilled to bits, captain Tony Jacklin takes centre stage as the Ryder Cup is retained by Europe in 1989, after a dogged fight by the Americans that ensured a tied match

Monitoring events with wife Astrid amid the mounting tension at the Belfry

Britain and Ireland a Ryder Cup tie. The following summer he joined the select group to have won the two premier Opens of golf.

If Lytham 1969 had made him a national sporting hero, then Hazeltine, Minnesota propelled Jacklin to true superstar status. An OBE was just one of the awards showered on him after that runaway seven strokes demolition of the best of American golf. It was the first in the USA for 50 years by a British golfer. Only Ted Ray and Jersey's Harry Vardon among Britons had hitherto won both titles.

Jacklin had secured his fortune and on his success the foundations of today's thriving European circuit were built, yet sadly he was never able to recapture the glory of that astonishing 12 months.

The first setback came when he started the defence of his Open title at St Andrews in 1970 by going out in a stunning 29 strokes and started the inward half with another birdie. Then a cloudburst ended play for the day. When Jacklin resumed the next morning the magic had gone, and although he finished fifth behind Jack Nicklaus, a golden chance had escaped. Another certainly did at Muirfield in 1972 where a combination of cruel luck and Lee Trevino's wizardry with a wedge denied him another Open. Their last day duel had the crowds agog and another home win looked likely when Jacklin struck three copybook strokes at the par five 71st. Trevino was still not on the green after four shots. Two putts from Jacklin looked certain to be enough to give him the lead and take him to the last needing a regulation four to overtake Nicklaus who had finished just ahead with a 66. Yet Trevino chipped in for his par and went on to win for the second year running, as Jacklin three-putted for a six. He was later to admit that incident had left him 'numb with shock'.

Although he won further domestic tournaments Jacklin was no longer a force in Championship golf. His future glories were to lie in leadership, a task he performed brilliantly in making Europe the strongest force in World golf.

CAREER HIGHLIGHTS

Major titles

British Open: 1969

US Open: 1970

Worldwide victories 25

Other achievements

Ryder Cup: 1967-69-71-73-75-77-79

Captain 1983-85-87-89

World Cup: 1966-70-71-72

Leading money-winner Europe: 1973

Bernhard Langer

Plagued by putting problems and a lack of self-confidence, Bernhard Langer experienced long periods in the doldrums — but he demonstrated his determination by winning the US Masters.

Shades of the past... or perhaps looking forward to the future? Bernhard Langer set about reconstructing his putting grip and found great success in 1990

No golfer has shown greater determination to be a champion than Bernhard Langer. Twice afflicted by the dreaded 'yips' in the early stages of his professional career, he then suffered the humiliating experience of being jeered during a British Open championship for his fumbling efforts to get the ball into the hole with his putter. A consoling thought for Langer must be that most golfers find their nerve on the greens deteriorates in middle age. An involuntary twitch of the muscles takes over and the four foot putt that was once a near formality is jerked uncontrollably wide of the target.

Langer's first attack came at 18, the second at 25, and the third six years later during the 1988 Open at Royal Lytham. While his long-time rival Seve Ballesteros was marching to the glory of a third Open title, Langer was publicly suffering after needing five putts to hole out from eight feet on the 17th green. The sages nodded sympathetically. In the eyes of most experienced judges he was a terminal case. The bricklayer's son from Augsburg, near Munich, once again proved them all wrong, finding yet another antidote by switching to a longer shafted putter. He took the twitch out of his putting action by grasping the putter grip with his left hand, then clamping the long shaft against his left arm by wrapping his right hand around his left wrist. The purists winced at the ugliness of this unorthodox method, but it has underpinned Langer's treasured place among the world's best.

Bernhard, who was born on 27th August

Using the unorthodox left-handed putting grip at the 1985 US Masters and (below) proving it a success as he is presented the Green Jacket by Ben Crenshaw

1957, has also had his determination tested by persistent back trouble but, like his putting affliction, has overcome it through sheer force of character. He started in golf as a caddy, turning professional at 15, but struggled with his putting until winning the 1979 World Under-25 title by a 17-stroke margin. Then, while on a visit to Britain, he took a fancy to a ladies putter and in 1980 became the first German to win a European tour event, with a 14 under par romp to the prestigious and highly popular Dunlop Masters at St Pierre.

The following season Langer was number one in Europe and again in 1984 when he won four times. The United States beckoned and he followed the trail blazed by Ballesteros. By then the 'yips' had returned, but after much experiment he decided on the simplest of solutions. For long-range putts he used the orthodox grip, for those under six feet he placed left hand below right and made the critics squirm.

That style took him to the ranks of the superstars in 1985 when he won the US Masters and the following week the Sea Pines Heritage Classic. Langer's triumph at Augusta came after two closing rounds of 68 gave him a two-shot margin over Ballesteros, Ray Floyd and Curtis Strange. He followed up at Harbour Town with an extra-time victory over Bobby Wadkins. He hit the high spots again in 1987 with brilliant wins in the PGA Championship at Wentworth, and the Irish Open. Many times winner of the German Closed title, he added his own German Masters promotion to his four German Open titles in 1989 and also took the Spanish Open.

A major contributor to Europe's Ryder Cup successes — he played in all in five matches in the 1980s — Langer crowned another fine year in 1990, during which he won in Madrid and Austria, by partnering Torsten Giedeon to a magnificent World Cup victory at Orlando. He proudly took the trophy home to stand alongside the soccer crown his countrymen had won in Rome some five months earlier.

Dazzling the Orlando faithful as he chips his way to a splendid World Cup victory in 1990

CAREER HIGHLIGHTS

Major titles

US Masters: 1985

Worldwide victories 29

Other achievements

Leading money-winner European tour: 1981-84

Ryder Cup: 1981-83-85-87-89

World Cup: 1976-77-78-79-80-90 (winner with Torsten Giedeon)

SANDY LYLE

Enthralling one moment, and frustrating the next, Sandy Lyle has nevertheless captured the hearts of many. On his day, the flying Scotsman could be virtually unbeatable, producing an array of winners from any part of the golf course.

'Och nou, yer canna buy talent!' Sandy in jovial mood

Most golfers are well acquainted with the peaks and troughs of the ancient game. Few have experienced the extremes of agony and ecstasy in such a short time as Sandy Lyle. His roller-coaster ride has been all the more poignant in that the ecstasy came first when he became Open champion in 1985, then later Britain's first winner of the US Masters in 1988.

When Scotland's Alexander Walter Barr Lyle struck a 7-iron bunker recovery some 145 yards to within ten feet of Augusta's final flag, and then sank the putt to win by one stroke, he joined the heavenly angels. His celebration shimmy as the ball sped into the centre of the hole was joyous theatre, the most dramatic finale yet to this showcase of the world's premier practitioners.

Already a four-time winner in the USA, the Shropshire lad had confirmed what his admirers had anticipated throughout the 1980s — that he had a rare talent that simply needed the right setting to be expressed. Most championships are decided by who makes the fewest mistakes or who is in the best position to take advantage of rivals' lapses. Augusta 1988 was notable for Lyle's brilliant winning move, golf's version of game, set, and match.

He had worked hard that April afternoon to force himself into position for that final birdie thrust despite having led second-placed Mark Calcavecchia by two shots at the start of the last round. With eight holes remaining Lyle led by four, but then dropped three shots to the card around Amen Corner against the American's two

One of the longest hitters in world golf, Sandy Lyle reached the pinnacle of his profession in the mid-1980s, but then came problems with his swing

birdies and a par to fall one behind.

Lyle retrieved that with a swinging 15 foot putt with a two-foot borrow across the green at the short 16th, and came to the last knowing he needed a par four to force a play-off with Calcavecchia who had finished ahead. When Lyle selected his one-iron for safety, but then hit his ball 250 yards into the fairway bunker, the British supporters present feared the worst. There can have been few moments as exciting for them or for millions of armchair sports fans as those that followed on that special day.

Lyle had joined the ranks of Major winners in much less spectacular style at Sandwich three years earlier. His game looked ideally suited to the unforgiving Royal St George's links, although that year's Open was as dull as the desolate terrain. Yet he took a long time to assert himself in an event in which nobody got to grips with the examination. There were half a dozen likely winners until Lyle holed a huge putt to birdie the long 14th. He birdied the next as well, and won by a stroke despite fluffing a greenside chip to bogey the last. Almost any one of his nine previous European victories had been more impressive, and the quality of his golf on the US tour in the 1980s most certainly came into that category.

Lyle had been swinging a club almost as soon as he could walk, and had been taught by his father Alex, who had moved south to become the professional at the Hawkstone Park club. Sandy was born in Shrewsbury on 9th February 1958. He was a brilliant schoolboy golfer, won an England Boys cap at 14, and in 1975 achieved the distinction of becoming the first to represent England at boy, youth and senior level in the same

The 1985 British Open and another successful birdie putt for Sandy...

season. He turned professional after playing in the 1977 Walker Cup, won the European Tour qualifying school and was Rookie of the Year in 1978. He was European Number One in the next two seasons, and again in his Open year of 1985.

Lyle's first American success was in the 1984 Kapalua International in Hawaii although it was not then a tour event. His first official success came two years later at Greensboro in North Carolina and the following season he captured the US Tournament Players Championship at Sawgrass in Florida. At the start of 1988 he won the Phoenix Open, then Greensboro again the week before his Masters triumph. Only Ballesteros among Europeans has won more events in the USA.

A first World Matchplay victory saw Lyle end 1988 on a high note , but 1989 proved a disastrous summer. Lyle's game deteriorated rapidly after a promising start to his next American tour campaign in which he twice finished second and had a third in early West Coast tournaments.

The realisation that there was something fundamentally wrong came when he failed to survive the halfway cut in his Masters defence, and was also eliminated after two rounds of the US Open. By mid-August he was forced to telephone Ryder Cup captain Tony Jacklin and beg to be excused from European duty against the USA at the Belfry. He ended the year in 53rd place in the European money list, his worst placing in 12 professional seasons.

Sandy's slide continued throughout 1990 as he sought a variety of advice on his swing problems. Eventually he joined the Leadbetter academy, following in the footsteps of old rival Faldo. Although he fell another six places in the rankings, and more or less decided he would not return to the US tour until 'cured' there were signs in the autumn that his torment was coming to an end. His greatest asset on the road to recovery may well be the serenity of his temperament. He has always been able to accept triumph and disaster as they come, and knows he faces a long, lonely slog on the comeback trail.

...and that elusive Open championship trophy is finally his!

CAREER HIGHLIGHTS

Major titles
British Open: 1985
US Masters: 1988

Worldwide victories 23

Other achievements
Ryder Cup: 1979-81-83-85-87
Walker Cup: 1977
World Cup: 1979-80
Leading Money winner Europe: 1979-80-85
World Matchplay: 1988

Johnny Miller

Majestic Johnny Miller thrilled the golfing world with his perfectly synchronised swing and rifling iron shots. The blond physical education graduate was a leading money-winner in 1974, before his star waned in the eighties.

It's looking good for Johnny as he reigns over golf in the mid-70s

From 1973 to 1976 Johnny Miller was the brightest star in the golf galaxy, at his peak a truly awesome player. Although the tall, blond physical education graduate from Brigham Young University turned professional in 1969, his arrival on the World stage can be pinpointed to the final round of the US Open at Oakmont, Philadelphia in June four years later. Majestic Miller had his long, flowing swing perfectly synchronised that Sunday when he started out six strokes behind the leaders on one of the hardest golf courses in America. He demolished it with a 63, still the lowest last round in any Major championship. It was his only victory that season but the following year saw Miller dominate the American circuit with a brand of golf that for consistent excellence still remains unsurpassed.

He won the first three tournaments of 1974, the Bing Crosby, Phoenix and Tucson Opens, then followed up with the Heritage and Tournament of Champions to take his victories to five in the first eleven events. Miller gave his rivals a respite by taking an extended break from the tournament scene, but then came back to finish the year with eight wins, as well as succeeding in Japan's Dunlop Phoenix. It was a phenomenal performance that easily made him leading money winner with a then record US$353,000 to be put in the bank. 'I feel I can win every week,' he would say. 'All I can do is keep trying my best.'

The following Spring Miller was away to another fast start in the Arizona desert, again winning in Phoenix and Tucson. He

Colour coordinating attire combined with an enthusiastic approach brought Johnny Miller a huge following

Petersburg Open, the first of his 21 US tour victories

shot a 61 in both tournaments, winning by 14 and nine strokes with totals of 24 and 25 under par, scoring that has never been bettered in the USA in consecutive tournaments. He finished 1975 with four victories, but just failed to take the Masters for which he started a hot favourite. Miller made a desultory start but then caught fire among the azaleas and dogwood to close with rounds of 65 and 66 which included six birdies in a row for an outward 30 to break all standing Augusta records. The title went to Jack Nicklaus for a fourth time but Miller was joint second with Tom Weiskopf a mere one stroke behind.

By the start of 1976 Miller had become a million-dollar money winner at the age of 28, although his religious convictions were always more important to him than the pursuit of personal wealth. Miller was born on 29th April 1947 in San Francisco, was raised in the Mormon Church and introduced to golf by his father Larry who was looking for a way for Johnny to get over the death of his elder brother who had tragically drowned in a fishing accident.

Johnny proved a natural and at 17 won the US Junior Championship, then qualified and finished eighth as an amateur in his first US Open at San Francisco's Olympic club. Miller's long hitting and rifling high iron shots were ideally suited to the 1976 heatwave at Royal Birkdale and he overhauled the precocious Ballesteros before speeding away to a six-stroke Open victory with a final round of 66.

Just as rapidly his star waned and, though he continued to win spasmodically on the US tour during the 1980s, the bogeys he had kept off his card with such ease in his heyday became all too frequent. His family — he has six children — and golf course architecture and golf club design now occupy most of his time along with his religious faith.

CAREER HIGHLIGHTS

Major titles
US Open: 1973
British Open: 1976

US Tour victories 23

Other achievement
Leading money-winner US Tour: 1974
Ryder Cup: 1975-81
World Cup: 1973-75-80
Individual winner: 1973-75

LARRY NELSON

A late starter to the game of golf, the unassuming American Larry Nelson found he had a natural talent and utilised it to claim 10 US tour victories along with two Majors in an often glittering career.

Nelson is down and out after the chip that got away in the Ryder Cup

Flamboyance is not an epithet that could readily be applied to the golf of Larry Nelson, but opponents who disregard the qualities of this unassuming American do so at their peril. Both Seve Ballesteros and Tom Watson did and paid the penalty, and Nelson's three Major titles remain convincing proof that patience and persistence more often than not gain the highest awards.

For a triple champion Nelson had a curious start to his career. Born on 10th September 1947 and brought up in Georgia, he did not begin playing the game until he was 21. He taught himself the mechanics of the swing by reading instruction books, particularly *Modern Fundamentals of Golf* by Ben Hogan. He became an assistant professional at a club in Georgia from where he qualified to join the US Tour in 1973. Despite a compact, smooth swing Nelson had to wait until 1979 for his first victory but then covered himself in glory in a remarkable Ryder Cup debut at The Greenbrier in West Virginia. That was the first match in which European golfers were

included and Europe's spearhead was Open champion Ballesteros. Nelson beat him 3 and 2 in the singles, twice in fourballs, again in foursomes, and the American ended with five wins out of five. Two years later as a member of probably the strongest US team to visit Britain, Nelson had another 100 per cent record with four wins at Walton Heath. Not until 1987 did the Europeans force Nelson to bow the knee, when Ballesteros and Olazabal claimed him in the opening foursomes at Muirfield Village.

Nelson's first Major came in his home town of Atlanta in 1981 when he took the US PGA by four strokes. He captured it again in 1987 at the PGA National course at Palm Beach after a play-off with Lanny Wadkins.

The performance which best illustrates Nelson's consistency under fire came in the 1983 US Open at Oakmont, where Johnny Miller had performed such last-day heroics ten years earlier. Nelson went into the championship playing poorly, having failed to win money in more than half his 16 tournaments that year. Opening rounds of 75 and 73 put him in 25th place — well back from the duel between Ballesteros and Watson at the head of affairs. All of a sudden Nelson found his form, collected seven birdies in the space of 11 holes, and handed in a 65 to trail the two giants by a stroke after the the events of the third round.

Nelson played the first nine holes of the final round in 33 but lost ground as Watson charged out in 31 to a 36 from Ballesteros. It looked all over, but Watson began to fritter strokes on the homeward run, and then the weather intervened. Watson was facing a ten-yard putt on the 14th, and Nelson his tee shot to the 230-yard 16th when a violent thunderstorm halted play for the day. When they came back on Monday morning Watson missed his putt and Nelson holed from fully 60 feet to birdie the short hole. He finished one ahead, having played the last 36 holes in 132, smashing a record in the process.

CAREER HIGHLIGHTS

Major titles
US Open: 1983
US PGA: 1981-87

US Tour victories 10

Other achievements
Ryder Cup: 1979-81-87

Staying calm in the face of adversity during the 1988 Masters at Augusta (opposite page) and surveying the scene later on that same year (left) at the British Open

Jack Nicklaus

With a record 20 Major championships under his belt and a list of credits unparalleled by anyone in the game, Jack Nicklaus has surely merited the title of 'The Greatest'.

Jack's three British Open victories guaranteed him a warm welcome on his visits to these shores

The dictionary definition of greatness is 'eminence in genius, ability, or power'. On all three counts Jack William Nicklaus, born in Columbus, Ohio on 21 January 1940 has been, and remains, superior to all his contemporaries over three complete decades. No one else can remotely challenge his total of 20 Major championships, and they will forever remain the yardstick by which future golfers and pretenders to the crown of 'The Greatest' will be judged.

The Golden Bear played his first national tournament as a schoolboy in 1953 and he has been breaking records ever since. In 1988 Nicklaus was named 'Player of the Century' and few contest that he is the greatest golfer the game has ever seen. The name of Nicklaus first went into the record books in 1959 when he won the first of two US Amateur titles, and British golf fans first saw him as a member of the victorious American Walker Cup team at Muirfield. While still an amateur he was runner-up to Arnold Palmer the following year in the US Open in Denver, and was also the individual winner of the World Team Championship. A second US Amateur title followed in 1961 to leave the golf world in no doubt that a brilliant new star was in the ascendancy.

Bobby Jones, whom Nicklaus had adopted as his hero, was one of the first to recognise that. Founder of the Masters at Augusta, Jones had watched Nicklaus make his debut in the US Amateur at the age of 15. 'It was not difficult to see that a new talent of the first magnitude had arrived,' he later wrote. Jones had won 13 Majors, seven professional and six amateur, to become a legend that even Walter Hagen and Ben Hogan had been unable to overshadow. Nicklaus caught his idol when he won his third US Open in 1972 and sailed into uncharted waters when he won a third US PGA victory the following summer.

Twenty seven years after his first Major

Putting the sand-iron to work with a peach of a shot

in 1959, Nicklaus won the Masters for a record sixth time at the age of 46 years and two months, to take his total of Majors to an unapproachable 20.

His irresistible rise to the peak of his profession had begun with his first professional victory — the US Open of 1962 — in which he had beaten Palmer in an 18-hole play-off, and by the time he began his 50th year his total of worldwide victories had reached an astonishing 91.

His third British Open triumph in 1978 saw him win all four of the modern Grand Slam events for the third time. One other staggering statistic marks the chronicle of Nicklaus' supremacy over the last 25 years.

He has finished second in a Major almost as many times as he has won. In 1964 he was runner-up in the British Open (to Tony Lema), the Masters (to Arnold Palmer) and the US PGA (to Bobby Nichols). There are 19 seconds to his credit in Majors and more than twice as many top ten finishes. There can be no greater tribute to the enduring consistency of the Nicklaus game which began as one of awesome power but soon evolved to one of masterly strategy.

In his early days the chunky Ohio college boy simply overwhelmed a golf course with huge hitting. Few greens were out of reach in two shots, and he was usually attacking the flags with two or three clubs less than his rivals. As the young Nicklaus was also a superb putter, and clearly relished the big occasion, he was soon enjoying a reputation as the amateur the professionals feared. Nicklaus hit the ball so hard that the insert on the face of his driver frequently burst. The Macgregor Company, which he later purchased, started putting six screws into

Jack drives powerfully down the fairway. Notice the distinctive interlocking grip on the shaft

the face of their woods instead of the usual four. Yet along with the power, went a style and concentration that has been a source of inspiration to generations of amateurs and professionals. Nicklaus was also among the first to use yardage charts, leaving nothing to chance in his course management.

He has always been willing to pass on his 'secrets', and he has written a small library of instruction books, and contributed to numerous videos. What he cannot impart are his own natural gifts and appetite for hard work that has made him the champion of champions. Nicklaus has been, and remains, successful at almost everything he has attempted. He is a first-class fisherman, a competent skier, and above average tennis player. Nowadays he is fast establishing a similar eminence as a golf course architect. His own creation at Muirfield Village, Ohio was the venue for the 1987 Ryder Cup. Nicklaus was captain of the American team, but that was one major encounter when the Bear did not enjoy a monopoly of success. Europe under Tony Jacklin gained their first Cup victory on US soil.

Those who also surmised that it marked the close of the Nicklaus era proved, not for the first time, to be making a hasty judgment. Nicklaus had confounded the critics with his 1986 Masters victory when his last round 65 gave him a one-stroke victory over his close friend and near-neighbour Greg Norman. Despite being the first to win $1 million on the US tour, and founder member of the two, three, four and five million dollar clubs, Nicklaus had still not finished setting new targets. In 1990 he made his debut on the US Senior tour, and won his first tournament to show that the fires of competition still burn as fiercely as ever. Six Masters, five US PGA titles, four US Opens, and three British Opens make Jack Nicklaus truly the Golfer of the Century. As a player he has only one remaining ambition — to become the first man to win a Major championship in his fifties.

Whatever currency you favour — whether pound, dollar or ECU — do not bet a single unit against Jack William Nicklaus doing just that.

Father and son line up a crucial putt at Augusta

CAREER HIGHLIGHTS

Major titles

20 British Open: 1966-70-78

US Open: 1962-67-72-80

US Masters: 1963-65-66-72-75-86

US PGA: 1963-71-73-75-80

US Amateur: 1959-61

Worldwide victories 71

Other achievements

Ryder Cup: 1969-71-73-75-77-81

Captain 83-87

Walker Cup: 1959-61

World Cup: 1963-64-65-66-67-71-73

Player of the Year: 1967-72-73-75-76

Leading US money-winner: 1964-65-67-71-72-73-75-76

World Matchplay: 1970

Greg Norman

Style-enthusiast Greg Norman should have won more than one Major championship given his undoubted flair and ability. Perhaps the nineties will see the Great White Shark fulfill those ambitions.

Grabbing the limelight at Turnberry in 1986 with his Open triumph

He could have been a Test cricketer or a fighter pilot. Instead Gregory John Norman found fame and fortune as a professional golfer and the leading international superstar of the 1980s. His journey from the backyards of Brisbane to his Florida haven has been a triumphant rocket ride for the flaxen-haired Queenslander the game knows as the Great White Shark.

Norman is charisma with a capital C , the golfer whose power and presence can elevate even a mundane tournament into a show-biz extravaganza. He is also a great enigma, winner of more than 60 tournaments around the globe, but so far only one of the Major championships.

That came in a truly memorable 1986, when he produced one of the great rounds in the 120-year history of the Open in shooting 63 to lift the title at Turnberry. That season he won ten times around the World, and was in the lead going into the last round of all four Majors.

Norman has gone on perplexing all those who recognise his talent but fail to understand why it has not brought him more titles. In 1987 he was beaten in a play-off for the Masters when Larry Mize holed an outrageous chip and run. That evoked memories of Bob Tway's last green bunker shot which flew straight into the hole and prevented the Australian winning the US PGA at Inverness the previous year. Then in 1989 he had both hands on a second Open when he shot a last round 64 to tie with Wayne Grady and Mark Calcavecchia and led in the play-off before blundering to let in

Greg manufactures a crafty escape from a bunker

the American for an eventual victory.

That lapse had people recalling those blocked second shots to the last hole of the 1984 US Open which he lost on a play-off to Fuzzy Zoeller, and the 1986 Masters where he finished a stroke behind Jack Nicklaus. Again in 1989 Norman had a bogey five at Augusta's last to miss joining the Nick Faldo/Scott Hoch play-off by one stroke. Nevertheless, he has been at the head of the Sony World rankings for all but a few weeks since they began in 1986, and he ended the 1990 season by topping the US money list for the second time.

It was another year of remarkable consistency on the most competitive of the world's circuits and included a typical Norman smash-and-grab act in the Doral Ryder Open in Miami. He shot a final round 62 to shatter the course and tournament record and tie with Paul Azinger, Calcavecchia and Tim Simpson. Then, amazingly, he chipped in for an eagle on the first play-off hole.

It was just one more example of Norman's duel with a destiny that did not have its beginnings until he was almost 16. Born at Mount Isa on 10 th February 1955, his first introduction to the game was as a caddy for his mother. He reckoned that if she could play pretty well it was worth while him giving it a try. Within two years he was down to scratch and had become Queensland junior champion. He turned professional in preference to an offer from the Australian Air Force, won his first Australian tournament in 1976, and his first in Britain on his debut in the Martini event at Blairgowrie the following summer.

Norman quickly became a prolific winner

Back on more familiar home soil at the 1989 Australian Open

both in Europe and Australia, being the former's top money winner in 1980 and Order of Merit leader in 1982. Having served his apprenticeship he committed himself full time to the USA in 1983 where he rapidly became one of the biggest attractions on a circuit sliding towards uniformity. It took him only three years to pass the million-dollar prize money milestone, and he was fastest to the two and three million marks. In 1990 the Shark's appetite was assuaged by a further $1.14 million, although nine wins in eight US seasons remains a meagre return.

Therein lies the reason why questions about Norman's right to a place among the greats of the modern game are so frequently posed. His ability to strike a golf ball, especially with the driver, is not in doubt and he is one of the fortunate few players who can generate genuine excitement. But the ones you don't win, especially the Majors, don't count. Norman has had too many near misses to be comfortable.

It is a paradox which to his credit he recognises and can confront. 'I'm due for at least two Majors to make up for the past,' he says. 'But over the long haul the breaks have a way of evening out, assuming that you are tough enough to hang in and keep playing hard. That's just what I plan to do.'

The world of golf needs an aggressive Greg Norman. He wins with flair and loses in style, without complaint. He is also a genuinely nice guy. He still has several years in which to put the record straight in the Majors, although it seems he will now have to carefully husband his resources. Norman has more than one painful memory to contend with, having learnt that the wrist injury he suffered during the 1988 US Open at Brookline will not heal of its own account. While playing the ninth in the second round he struck a rock beneath his ball. The blow gave him a severe jolt and put him out of action for two months. Surgery is a risk, so he will have to live with the pain. He will regard that as a small price to pay for just one Masters or US Open victory.

CAREER HIGHLIGHTS

Major titles

British Open: 1986

Worldwide victories 67

Other achievements

World Cup: 1976-78

Leading US money-winner: 1986-90

Leading money-winner in Europe: 1982

World Matchplay: 1980-83-86

Will US Major success continue to elude Greg Norman, or will the nineties see the Aussie overcome the psychological barriers that have dogged his career?

Jose Maria Olazabal

As the brightest young star to emerge in the eighties, Jose Maria Olazabal showed great maturity in winning the World series at Akron at the start of the nineties.

Checking the borrow at Muirfield Village during the 1987 Ryder Cup (below) and a short-iron shot to the 14th green (opposite) at the Golf del Sur, Tenerife in 1989

Few young men have made such an impact on the World golf scene as the greenkeeper's son from Fuenterrabia in north west Spain. By the time the slender 17-year old arrived at Scotland's Glenbervie club for the 1983 British Boy's championship word had already spread of an astonishing new talent. With his own and Italy's senior national titles already to his credit, Jose Maria romped away with the title , winning 6 and 5 against France's Marc Pendaries.

The next year Olazabal, born on 5th February 1966, was back to win the Amateur Championship at Formby where a bewildering array of spectacular shots, including a hole-in-one, accounted for Scotland's Colin Montgomerie. Then in 1985 he became the first and so far only player to perform the Amateur hat-trick, capturing the Youth title at Ganton.

When he turned professional that autumn and immediately won the European Tour qualifying school it was clear that Europe had unearthed someone who could also scale the heights attained by the illustrious Ballesteros. 'Ollie' did not disappoint in his first professional season,

winning the European Masters, Swiss Open and the Sanyo title in Barcelona to finish second in the Order of Merit and make the Rookie of the Year award a formality. Although he did not have a victory in 1987 he had already done enough to assure himself of being one of captain Tony Jacklin's personal choices for the Ryder Cup match at Muirfield Village in 1987.

However, it was his 1990 performances that underlined his potential to be one of the dominant figures of the new decade. Olazabal scored his first British professional win in the Benson and Hedges International, then took the Irish Open in Dublin and the Lancome Trophy in Paris.

In August he stayed on after the US PGA Championship and shook Americans rigid with a 12-stroke victory in the World Series at Akron, Ohio. Olazabal demolished the ferocious Firestone course with a first-round 61 and followed with a trio of 67s for a stunning 18 under par total of 262. Not since Tony Jacklin led after each round at Chaska to win the US Open by seven strokes had any overseas golfer made such an impact. Olazabal later described that week as 'four days when I was perfectly coordinated. My ball striking was as good as I could play, and my putting was very nearly my best.'

He ended the year with another win in Japan to take his career winnings to £2 million. Olazabal's record in the four Majors was second only to Faldo during 1989 and 1990, which ended with his elevation to third place in the world rankings At Augusta in 1991, he came within one shot of winning the US Masters, and it will surely be only a matter of time before a Major championship comes his way.

Jose has become the leading European light on the US circuit, and here he is deftly chipping onto the green during the 1990 US PGA at Shoalcreek

CAREER HIGHLIGHTS

Major titles
Nil

Worldwide victories 12
(European Tour, 9)

Other achievements
World Series: 1990
Visa Taiheiyo Masters (Japan): 1989-90
Ryder Cup: 1987-89
World Cup: 1989
Dunhill Cup: 1986-87-88-89

Arnold Palmer

The growls and grins made him human. His powerful driving and clever putting inspired the golf boom in the sixties. The legendary Arnold Palmer will never be forgotten.

The millionaires of the modern game owe an eternal debt of gratitude to Arnold Palmer. Several outstanding golfers, Walter Hagen and Henry Cotton among them, had previously acquired a dedicated following for their showmanship and skill. Hagen's taste for the good life had helped to give the professional golfer respected status in society. Cotton had been Britain's answer to the American's flamboyance and had topped the bill at the London Palladium, amusing the patrons with trick shots and golfing anecdotes. But the arrival of Arnold Daniel Palmer on the golf scene coincided with a sudden expansion of television, and the combination was sensational. Palmer's devil-may-care attitude to championship golf, his rugged good looks, and the sheer power of his game instantly struck a chord with the sporting public. Whether it was back home in Latrobe, Pennsylvania, throughout the USA or in Britain and the Continent, Palmer was idolised.

Born in 1929 — his father was a steelworker before becoming a golf professional — Palmer had huge hands and a heart to match. He possessed a charisma given to few, and perhaps only Severiano Ballesteros of today's household names has emulated his universal appeal.

Palmer 's characteristic twirl at the top of his follow-through represented the final flourish to a ferocious onslaught on the ball. When that failed to go where he had intended he extricated himself from trouble with a series of scarcely believable recovery shots. Along with the strokeplay went the

'Yippee!' Delight on Arnie's face after holing a difficult putt at the US Open in 1960

Launching into a drive on the Seniors tour (opposite), astride chief protagonist Nicklaus (left) and having a few welcome puffs between holes (below) at the US Open in 1966

growls and grins that gave this most human of golfers his massive public appeal. The golf boom began in the 1960s when Palmer's exploits, brought into the living room by the small screen, gave golf to the masses. Hitherto it had been restricted to those who played or were members of private clubs.

Palmer's arrival in Britain for the 1960 Centenary Open at St Andrews started a revival of popularity for the Championship among overseas players leading to today's justifiable claim that it is the true World Championship of Golf. He arrived at the home of golf as Masters and US Open champion, and his target was to match Hogan's feat in not only winning three Majors in one year, but also to take the Open at his first attempt. The Texan had completed the hat-trick in 1953.

Palmer was to narrowly fail, beaten by one stroke by Australia's Kel Nagle, despite a last-round 68. However, he returned the following year at Royal Birkdale, defeated everyone and the wild weather, and successfully defended the title at Troon in 1962, beating Nagle by six strokes. Two wins and a second in his first three British Opens remains a record unmatched.

Palmer has eight majors to his credit, starting with the 1954 US Amateur title. He also took the Masters in 1958, 1962 and 1964.

It's all in the footwear ...never mind the knock-knees!

Although his fourth US Masters was his last Major success, Palmer kept on winning tournaments all round the world well into the 1970s. He captained the US Ryder Cup team of 1975, leading it to victory at Laurel Valley in his home State. In 1963 he had been playing captain of the victorious American team at Atlanta. It was also in 1975 that Palmer evoked memories of his Open performance at Birkdale in 1961 when he won the European PGA title at Sandwich in a gale. While the rest of the field were being blown to sixes and sevens, Palmer, then 46, beat the elements with his one-iron to conjure a par round from the Royal St George's links.

Yet he was far more than just a powerhouse from the tee. In his heyday Palmer was an inspired putter. He had a distinctive knock-kneed stance that benefited him most in the wind, keeping his body and head still. He went boldly for every putt, seemingly convinced he would sink those especially nasty three-feet returns.

A hitch of his trousers in moments of stress was a Palmer trademark, as was the glove protruding, fingers first, from his hip pocket. His magnetism made him a fortune from golf, and he is still winning money on the US Seniors tour that he joined full-time in 1980. As well as being the 'father' of the modern golf superstar, Palmer was also the generator that enabled super-agent Mark McCormack to build his own vast empire.

They had been fellow students at Wake Forest University, playing in the same golf team before McCormack went on to law school. When they re-united McCormack made his reputation by marketing Palmer throughout the USA with brilliant success. Arnie's personality and good humour made that a relatively easy task, and McCormack was able to fulfil golf's need for hero-worship. Palmer was a perfect prototype.

CAREER HIGHLIGHTS

Major titles

British Open: 1961-62

US Open: 1960

US Masters: 1958-60-62-64

US Amateur: 1954

Worldwide victories 70

Other achievements

Ryder Cup: 1961-63-65-67-71-73

Captain 1963-75

World Cup: 1960-62-63-64-65-66-67

Seniors Tour: US Seniors Open 1981

Senior TPC 1985

Leading US money-winner: 1958-60-62-63

(in 1968 became the first American golfer to reach $1 million prize money)

World Matchplay: 1964-67

GARY PLAYER

In a distinguished career spanning over 30 years, Gary Player's tireless enthusiasm for the game, coupled with a do-or-die philosophy towards winning has earned him the respect of his contemporaries worldwide.

South Africa's man in black is living proof that fitness, determination and a fierce competitive instinct can turn any man into a champion. Gary Player is a natural athlete who has always kept himself in excellent physical condition, but he had to work twice as hard to turn himself into a golfer capable of competing with the best.

Born in Johannesburg on 1st November 1935, he was the son of a mine captain who introduced him to the game in his early teens. When he set out for Britain at the age of 20 to seek fame and fortune, Player was puny in comparison to most of his contemporaries. He stood just 5 ft 7 inches tall and barely weighed 10 stone. On top of that his technique was suspect, for he had a hooker's grip and a very flat swing. Moreover, his early experiences suggested that the critics were right and that he should look for an alternative career.

Player surprised everyone with the speed of his breakthrough to the winner's rostrum, and within the remarkably short space of four years had become Open champion. He went on to become the first overseas winner of the Masters, the first 'foreigner' to win the US Open since 1920, and still remains the only non-American to win all four of the World's Major championships.

Player won nine Majors spread over three decades — his first being the 1959 Open at Muirfield, his last being his third Masters in 1978, at the age of 42. It was one of his finest performances in a distinguished career as he birdied seven of the last ten holes, getting home in 30 for a last-round 64 to win by one

Gary Player has demonstrated a true professional's approach to the game of golf for three decades

Sporting his treasured chequered cap at the tee off

The supreme fitness fanatic, Player remains a high level competitor even now

stroke. Yet although Player was the first overseas professional to become a prolific winner in the USA, he was equally at home in every other continent. He has more than 130 victories to his credit worldwide and is still active on the US Seniors circuit where he has now been joined by the other members of the famous Big Three — Arnold Palmer and Jack Nicklaus.

It is a tribute to his fitness that Player is still a formidable force at the highest level of competition although inevitably his chances of becoming only the fourth man in history to win ten Majors are decreasing with each passing year. The South African's fitness fads have been a colourful part of the game's folklore. Believing that fruit was the key to a healthy body he used to arrange for a case of bananas to be delivered to his headquarters at every tournament. There was always a wide variety of fruit in his hotel room. Wheat-germ, burnt bacon, weight-lifting and yoga have been and remain other aids to conditioning. Player's preoccupation with such matters was all part of his determination to be stronger and better than the big men of golf. When he realised he did not have the power to match big-hitters like Nicklaus and Palmer, he consulted a body builder, made his clubs longer, and changed his swing to give himself the greater leverage that is the secret of long driving.

He would run miles to give himself the leg strength, and a daily programme of 100 finger-tip press-ups resulted in enormous upper body power for such a small man. One of his party tricks was to do press-ups on one arm, raising his body horizontally. If you think that is easy, just try it. Norman Vincent Peel's *Power of Positive Thinking* was Player's bible, and his trademark is still all black clothing. He believes that black absorbs the sun's rays and gives him extra strength. When he wasn't exercising or playing golf, Player practised. He is recognised as the finest bunker player in the game and he would spend hours on the practice ground, refusing to leave a trap until he had sunk three recoveries in a row. 'The more I practise the luckier I get' was his oft-repeated answer to those who had the temerity to question the value of such an excessive amount of voluntary overtime.

Player showed similar dedication when it came to adjusting his swing technique. He studied film of former champions such as Henry Cotton and Sam Snead in the hope of acquiring that extra fraction of knowledge that would give him an edge over his contemporaries. He found the answer to his problems after consulting Ben Hogan, the taciturn Texan who had recovered from a horrific car crash to win three Majors in 1953. Hogan diagnosed the reasons for

The classic swing in all its full glory during those halcyon days of the sixties

Player's ultra-flat swing, and suggested the modifications he should make. Thus armed, Player went out to confront the Goliaths of golf, and proved for almost 20 years that he was at the very least their equal. Although Player became synonymous with the World Matchplay Championship at Wentworth — and still holds the record of five victories — his finest British performance remains the 1974 Open at Royal Lytham. It was the first Open to be played with the 1.68 inch big ball. The South African twice broke 70 and won by four strokes during a week of wind and rain to demonstrate the superb quality of his strokeplay.

The triumph was not without drama, for in the last round Player found his ball in the greenside rough at the 17th with seconds to spare. With his customary attention to detail he had ensured he would not be penalised for exceeding the permitted five minutes search time by using a wristwatch. Then at the 72nd hole his approach ran through the green and finished too close to the clubhouse wall to permit him to play an orthodox recovery. Player executed his third shot from under the lounge windows of the clubhouse with a putter, wielded left-handed.

Gary Player, forever the showman, has never been short of imagination and flair on the stage of world golf!

CAREER HIGHLIGHTS

Major titles

British Open: 1959-68-74

US Open: 1965

US Masters: 1961-74-78

US PGA: 1962-72

Worldwide victories 134

Other achievements

World Cup: 1956-57-58-59-60-62-63-64-65-66-67-68-71-72-73-77

Seniors Tour: US Seniors Open 1987-88

Senior TPC 1987

British Seniors 1988-90

Leading US money-winner: 1961

World Matchplay: 1965-66-68-71-73

Payne Stewart

He may be known as 'The Peacock' in some quarters, but beneath Payne Stewart's appearance lies a gritty, determined and reliable golfer who finished third in the 1990 US Order of Merit table.

Throughout the 1980s Payne Stewart has established himself as one of the best of the new generation of American tournament golfers — and he is certainly the most instantly recognisable. Stewart's breakthrough to Major winner came, after several near misses, in the PGA Championship of 1989 by which time he was already well known around the world for his distinctive garb. The man from Orlando in Florida is the standard-bearer for the National Football League and sports the colours of its teams on his tournament forays. One day its the Bears, the next the Rams, Tigers or Dolphins.

Not since Max Faulkner enlivened a drab post-war British scene, has the golf world enjoyed such a technicolour kaleidoscope. Yet William Payne Stewart, born in Springfield, Missouri on 30th January 1957 is much more than an itinerant clothes horse as his record in the British Open reveals. Runner-up to Sandy Lyle at Sandwich in 1985, he was fourth behind Nick Faldo at Muirfield in 1987, then seventh and eighth on his next two attempts. In 1990 he was runner-up again, five strokes behind Nick Faldo at St Andrews. He ended the season by winning the World Cup individual title on his home course at Grand Cypress to add to the two victories he obtained on the US Tour. Runner- up to Tom Kite in 1989, he was third behind Greg Norman in the 1990 US Order of Merit table.

Stewart had a traditional American upbringing, graduating in business studies at the Southern Methodist University where he arrived on the customary golf scholarship. He turned professional in 1979, but learnt his trade on the Far East Asian circuit where he won the Indian and Indonesian Opens in 1981. While in Malaysia he met his wife Tracey. He qualified for the US tour at that autumn's school and won the Quad Cities Open and Walt Disney Classic in his first two seasons.

'Get in there, you sucker!' A vital birdie goes down at the 18th during the 1989 US PGA

Stewart's overseas experience — he also won in Australia — helped him to quickly forge a reputation as a strong, reliable player. He is now a devoted student of sports psychology, a subject which he believes is ignored by today's golfers. 'I used to set myself monetary goals,' he says, 'and I had to learn to set my own goals and learn to be in focus with myself.'

Stewart has now set his sights on further Major victories after joining the ranks of champions at Kemper Lakes in 1989. He showed he had the aggressive game and the temperament for the big occasion by taking advantage of mistakes by Mike Reid to secure his place in Raymond Floyd's Ryder

The Open 1990 and the niftiest dresser on the golf circuit parades his wares

A proud moment as Payne poses with the 1989 US PGA Championship trophy at Kemper Lakes, Chicago

Cup team. In some ways it was poetic justice, for Stewart might have won the 1986 US Open at Shinnecock Hills. He led with six holes to play, but then fluffed a chip and saw Floyd go on to take the title.

The Ryder Cup wasn't too kind to Payne either. Having beaten Jose Maria Olazabal on his Ryder Cup debut in 1987, but then seen the USA beaten for the first time at home, he lost to the Spaniard in the 1989 tie at the Belfry. That was one occasion when the Payne peacock could not crow, after finding a watery grave at the 18th.

CAREER HIGHLIGHTS

Major titles

US PGA: 1989

US Tour victories 7

Others achievements

Ryder Cup: 1987-89

World Cup: 1987-90

(Individual winner)

'Oft on a plat of rising ground, I hear the far-off curfew sound, over some wide-watered beach, swinging slowly but beyond the reach, of those who hear the lost, not found'. Pebble Beach, 1991

Curtis Strange

Curtis Strange is one of the most prolific earners in world golf, and this despite a reluctance in his earlier years to travel outside the US circuit. He has two US Open championships to his credit.

The 4th round of the US Open 1988, and Curtis takes to the towel as the pressure mounts

Despite a brilliant amateur career it took Curtis Northrup Strange a long tıme to establish himself as one of the greats of the modern game. The handsome Virginian found it a difficult transition to touring professional. He had to wait three years for his first victory and it was another nine before he captured his first Major title. Yet when he made the breakthrough it was in the event that matters most to an American, the US Open. His defeat of Britain's Nick Faldo in the 1988 Championship at Brookline confirmed Curtis as one of the most feared competitors of the modern game, and his successful defence the following year at Oak Hill shot him to superstar status. Those back-to-back wins made him the first since Ben Hogan in 1950-51 to take the US Open in successive years. Only four others, including Bobby Jones in 1929 and 1930, had achieved that amazing feat since the championship began back in those early days of 1895.

Strange and his twin brother Alan were born in Norfolk, Virginia on January 30th 1955, the sons of a golf professional who owned the White Sands country club in Virginia Beach. Both began playing the game at the age of seven and set themselves on an inevitable course towards a professional career. Alan did indeed become a member of the US Tour before giving up the game to go into business as a stockbroker. However it was Curtis who exhibited the greater talent and determination to succeed in golf and was soon making his mark when he enrolled at Arnold Palmer's alma mater Wake Forest University. Although he did not win the US Amateur title, he captured almost every other significant event including the South Eastern, the Western, the North and South, and the Eastern which his father had won 20 years before. He was American collegiate champion in 1974, also helped the USA win the World Amateur trophy, and then figured prominently in the victorious 1975 US

The master escape artist from the sandtraps

The 1988 US Open Champion celebrates with his wife

Walker Cup team at St Andrews.

During his formative professional years Curtis earned a reputation as a 'grinder', a steady performer who was always in the running and the money, but never the winner of a Major tournament. He contributed to that assessment by showing a reluctance to travel outside the comfortable confines of the US circuit which provided such a lucrative income. All that began to change in 1985 when he had a near miss in the Masters, won three times to become leading money winner in the US for the first time, and began to acquire a collection of stamps in his passport.

In 1987 he again scored three US tour victories and crowned them with the finest round ever played at the home of golf. In the Dunhill Cup at St Andrews he toured the Old course in only 62 strokes beating Australian Rodger Davis' 24-hour-old 63 with a birdie at the last as he got out and home in 31. That was one performance where money did not matter, and it gave Curtis a stature which he gloriously enhanced with those twin US Open victories. In 1988 he was the first American to bank more than $1 million prize money, thus stretching his career earnings since 1977 to an unbelievable $4 million plus, and the nineties promise even more.

CAREER HIGHLIGHTS

Major titles
US Open: 1988-89

US Tour victories 17
including Canadian Open: 1985-87
Memorial: 1988
Nabisco Champ: 1988
Leading money-winner US tour: 1985-87,88
US PGA Player of the year: 1988
Walker Cup: 1975
Ryder Cup: 1983-85-87-89
Dunhill Cup: 1987-88-89-90

Lee Trevino

As the kid from the wrong side of the tracks, Lee Trevino lived and breathed golf from the age of 14. He defied critics of his unorthodox swing by amassing five Majors ... and the passion remains.

Most of the leading American players of the last 25 years are the products of college golf. Nicklaus, Palmer, Watson, Miller and Strange are obvious examples of a seemingly endless production line. Lee Trevino has been the most notable exception, showing that a kid from the wrong side of the tracks can reach the very highest level if he has the skill and determination. It would take a book twice this size to describe all the exploits of the character the game reveres as Supermex, even though his professional tournament career did not begin until the relatively advanced age of 27.

The story of Lee Buck Trevino is one of the most colourful rags-to-riches sagas of any sport. He was born on the first day of December 1939, but never knew his father. Brought up in a shack in downtown Dallas, he left school at 14, and went to work at a local driving range before signing for a four-year stint in the US Marine Corps. As a teenager who never knew where the next dollar was coming from, he learnt all the tricks of the urchin caddie, and by the time he became a serviceman he could hustle with the best. He supplemented his Marine pay by giving lessons and regular beatings to officers, and when he came out in 1960 became an assistant in El Paso.

Lee was an inveterate gambler and made his living from playing money matches in between giving lessons to the local 'gentry'. He lived and breathed golf from dawn to dusk, developing his exceptional hand and eye coordination by playing his club's par three course — for money naturally — using

'Supermex' in a huff... but in reality playing up to the crowd after one that got away

a Coca-Cola bottle wrapped in adhesive tape to stop it shattering. Trevino would hit the ball baseball-style and then use the bottle like a snooker cue on the greens to putt out. He rarely lost, although those foolish enough to take him on were permitted to play with a full set of clubs.

When he qualified to play in the 1966 US Open, and finished 54th, Trevino was already a fine player with a unique swing. He developed his pronounced open address position as an anti-hooking device, having

'I only have eyes for you...' (above), and guns still blazing (right) on the Senior circuit

seen too many of his low flying shots disappear into the left rough alongside the bone-hard Texas fairways. It was, and remains, a classic slicer's stance and when Trevino won the 1968 US Open at Oak Hill, the critics and rival players were for once in agreement. He could not last, they said, with such a technique. Trevino, who had scored under 70 in all four rounds, proved them wrong of course, and within six years had won five Majors, his sixth coming in 1984 when he took the US PGA title for the second time at the age of 44.

When Trevino added the high fade shot that he had so admired in watching Ben Hogan to his repertoire he had the armoury to tackle any course. Technically his swing was not a pretty sight, but it enabled him to reproduce the required shot at will. It took Masters champion George Archer to state the obvious secret of Trevino's startling rise to stardom. 'The best golf swing is the one that repeats most often,' said Archer, 'and the swing that repeats most often is Lee

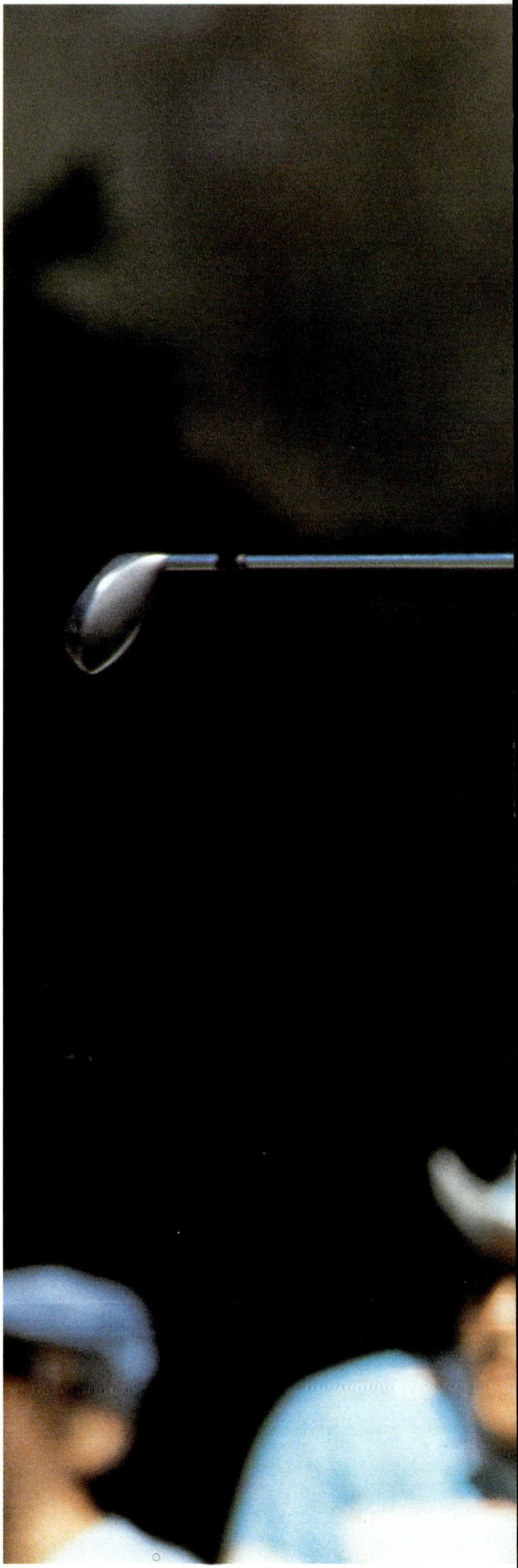

The 1984 US PGA Champion — and no doubt contemplating a major reconstruction of the old trophy cabinet!

Trevino's. It just simply repeats ... repeats ... and repeats ...'

His finest year was 1971 when in the space of five weeks he won the US Open at Merion, beating Jack Nicklaus in a play-off, the Canadian Open, then the British Open at Royal Birkdale. He was champion again at Muirfield in 1972, demonstrating his uncanny ability to produce the killer stroke at the right moment. Trevino broke Jacklin's heart in that Open duel, chipping in three times and also holing a bunker shot to wreck the hopes of the British golfer.

In 1974 he collected his first US PGA Championship but has never been able to complete the set with a Masters title. Whether it has been the struggle against constant back problems, aggravated when he was struck by lightning during the Western Open in Chicago in 1975, or his dislike of the Augusta course and atmosphere, may never be accurately assessed. Certainly Trevino has never been a force at the Masters, believing his game is unsuited to its demands.

Trevino had an operation for a herniated disc after the lightning bolt struck him at Butler National. 'I guess I learnt that day that when God wants to play through you stand aside', he quipped. He has gone on living up to his extrovert reputation, yet off the course Trevino remains a quiet, dedicated family man. He has won and lost fortunes, more than one business venture ending in disaster. In the 1980s he cut back on his tournament appearances to concentrate on television commentaries, until he became eligible for the Seniors Tour. That 50th birthday should have been the signal for Lee to take his foot off the accelerator marked ambition, but the competitive fires are still bright.

In 1990, his first Senior year, he topped the magic one million dollar prize money mark, and his third wife Claudia and their daughter Olivia Leigh now have all the security they require.

Trevino will go on playing golf as long as he remains competitive. He is now battling for new titles against old adversaries Nicklaus, Palmer and Player and often states: 'I have made my reservations for the British Open until I am 60.' He will never lack for a welcome in these shores.

CAREER HIGHLIGHTS

Major titles

British Open: 1971-72

US Open: 1968-71

US PGA: 1974-84

Worldwide victories 47

Other achievements

Ryder Cup: 1969-71-73-75-79-81

Captain 1985

World Cup: 1968-69-70-71-74

Seniors Tour, US Seniors Open: 1990

Leading US money-winner: 1970

LANNY WADKINS

No-nonsense go-for-broke golf was his hallmark. Lanny Wadkins would storm through the field with birdie after birdie, leaving opponents trailing in his wake.

Lanny and his merry band of followers getting fired up at the US PGA in 1984

Lanny Wadkins, whose younger brother Bobby is also a touring professional, has been at the forefront of American golf for 20 years, and his powers show little sign of diminishing. Winner of 19 US Tour events and with career earnings approaching US$5 million at the start of 1991, the Virginian's record could so easily have been even more impressive given more luck and the right set of circumstances on the day.

Only one Major, the 1977 US PGA championship, has fallen to his aggressive shot-making but he has had near misses in another four or five. He was runner-up for the US PGA title in 1982, 1984 and 1987, and runner-up for the US Open to Raymond Floyd in 1986.

Jerry Lanston Wadkins was born in Richmond on 5th December 1949 and was soon dominating junior golf in his home area, with Bobby also making his mark as a promising amateur. Lanny outstripped him to become a Walker Cup player in 1969 and 1971 and in between won the US Amateur championship. He won the Sahara

Flexing his muscles at the 1984 US PGA

Invitational on his way to finishing 10th in his first full season on the US circuit, and to his great delight was subsequently given the title of Rookie of the Year.

Two more victories followed in 1973 but another four years elapsed before he made the breakthrough everyone had been predicting. It came at Pebble Beach in California and Lanny was not the most popular of golfers when he snuffed out the fairytale hopes of 47-year-old Gene Littler, who had won the US Open back in 1961. Littler led by five shots with nine holes remaining, but Wadkins birdied the 18th to close with a 70 that was good enough to tie, and then went on to beat the veteran at the third play-off hole. He also took the World Series that year and made the first of six Ryder Cup appearances in the Golden Jubilee match at Royal Lytham. Wadkins won all three of his matches in an easy American victory that was destined to be the last time that Britain and Ireland would alone provide the opposition in that great clash of nations.

Wadkins' next outstanding victory came in the Tournament Players Championship at Sawgrass in 1979 when he defied a howling storm whipping up 45 mph winds to defeat the evergreen Tom Watson by five strokes. Seven times he has won twice in a season and in 1985, when he took the Bob Hope Desert Classic, the Los Angeles Open and the Walt Disney Classic to finish second in the money list, he was named PGA Player of the Year. Wadkins has kept on acquiring titles and in his 40th year claimed the Anheuser-Busch Classic at Williamsburg in his home state, although he now lives in Dallas. He completed 1990 in a creditable 13th place in the US Money ranking list with over US$670,000 from 23 appearances. The American also took time out to make a rare European appearance in the new Austrian Open at a picturesque Salzburg where he fought a tantalising 75-hole duel with Bernhard Langer before unfortunately losing to the German in a play-off. Once again Wadkins had thrilled the galleries with the no-nonsense go-for-broke style of golf that has been his hallmark.

Lanny sinks a crucial putt, determination etched all over his face

CAREER HIGHLIGHTS

Major titles
US PGA: 1977

US Tour victories 19

Other achievements
Ryder Cup: 1977-79-83-85-87-89
World Cup: 1977-84-85
Walker Cup: 1969-71

Tom Watson

True greatness is an elusive thing in sport. Tom Watson has touched those heights and has exhibited an insatiable appetite for championship titles throughout his career... but can he ever again rekindle the flame?

Royal Birkdale in 1983 was the setting for Tom Watson's fifth Open triumph and here he is looking pleased after a birdie putt while (opposite) the trophy is his

In the space of nine years from 1975 to 1983 Tom Watson became the dominant figure in golf on both sides of the Atlantic. In Britain he won five Open Championships, completing the full hand faster than any of the other four men who have achieved the feat, and arguably against much the fiercest opposition. Australian Peter Thomson who dominated the Open in the 1950s won his five titles between 1954 and 1965, while the Great Triumvirate of Braid, Vardon and Taylor took 10, 16, and 19 years respectively between 1894 and 1914. In the USA during his halcyon years the freckle-faced kid from Kansas City won the Masters in 1977 and 1981, and then the US Open after a third exciting duel with Jack Nicklaus . He was also leading money winner there four times in a row from 1977.

Watson, whose father Ray was a scratch golfer, was born on 4th September 1949 and was introduced to the game at an early age. By the time he was seven young Tom was playing regularly with his father and his friends, and at 13 was regularly beating them in the Saturday morning two-dollar Nassaus at the local club. That early introduction to competition was vital in honing the hunter's instinct which served Watson so well when he turned professional in 1971 after graduating in psychology from Stanford University in the USA.

His first tour win came in the Western Open of 1974, but by the time he arrived at Carnoustie for the following year's British Open, he had already been branded a 'choker' having lost two successive US Opens and that year's Masters from

Tom demonstrates a perfectly executed long-iron shot down the fairway

seemingly impregnable positions. Watson showed just how unfair and premature that verdict was by beating Australian Jack Newton in a play-off after he had birdied the 72nd to force a tie. Once he had made the breakthrough, Watson exhibited an insatiable appetite for titles.

Watson's crisp striking and no frills approach quickly endeared him to British golf fans. He rewarded their respect and affection by producing some of the finest golf ever seen on the great links of Britain. His best came at Turnberry in 1977 in what has become known as the 'Great Shoot Out'. Watson and Nicklaus fought a duel in the sun which no scriptwriter could have bettered. They traded shot for shot for all four days, the combination of stroke and matchplay enthralling the huge crowds. The outcome was in doubt until the final hole which Watson began one ahead having birdied the 71st. Nicklaus drove into the base of a gorse bush but smashed his recovery to the fringe of the green. Watson, only four feet from the hole in two strokes, watched his great rival hole from all of 15 yards for his birdie, then rolled in his own birdie putt to win by a shot. Fellow American Hubert Green who was third, ten shots behind Nicklaus, commented, 'There were two tournaments that week, and I won the "B" division.'

Three months earlier Watson and Nicklaus had fought out the 1977 Masters, the Golden Bear firing a final round of 66, but Watson responding with a 67 to take that title for the first time by two strokes. The World's best were in conflict once again in the 1982 US Open on the links at Pebble Beach. On that occasion Tom again birdied the final two holes to pip Jack again, the key shot coming at the short 17th, where, after missing the green, Watson chipped in. His joyous scamper round the green remains one of the most memorable moments of championship golf. For Nicklaus, watching on a television monitor beside the 18th green, it was another reminder that his best shots were no longer good enough.

Watson was to undergo a similar experience at St Andrews two years later, but before then he had triumphed at Muirfield in 1980, at Troon in 1982, then for a fifth time at Royal Birkdale in 1983.

Tom's sharpshooting at Muirfield, where he had a third round 64, took him to a comfortable four-stroke victory but there was an element of fortune about his next. Watson closed with a 70 for a 284 total and won by one stroke from Britain's Peter Oosterhuis and Zimbabwe's Nick Price. The latter needed par figures for the last six holes for victory, but the task was beyond him.

The man from Kansas had a tougher struggle at Birkdale, where half a dozen were in contention on the last day. That climaxed with Watson needing a par four at the last to hold off fellow Americans Hale Irwin and Andy Bean. He secured it with an imperious two-iron shot to find the target, and headed for St Andrews on a hat-trick. That 1984 Open saw Watson bow the knee to a new King, the charismatic Spaniard Severiano Ballesteros. Chasing a sixth Open to equal Vardon's record, Watson was unhinged at the dreaded Road Hole on the last day. He overclubbed with the same iron that had clinched his victory the previous year, and finished up against the boundary wall beyond the green. Almost simultaneously Ballesteros, up ahead, birdied the 18th and Watson's reign was over. His golf went downhill from then on, but a well earned third place in the 1991 US Masters at Augusta reconfirmed his position as one of the all-time greats in the game.

Ryder cup joy for Watson at the Belfry in 1989 as a putt goes down

CAREER HIGHLIGHTS

Major titles

British Open: 1975-77-80-82-83

US Open: 1982

US Masters: 1977-81

Worldwide victories 40

Other achievements

Ryder Cup: 1977-81-83-89

Leading US money-winner: 1977-78-79-80-84

Ian Woosnam

Ian Woosnam ended the 1990 season as the leading money earner in golf, with five European titles in his pocket. A Major championship continued to elude him... until one spring day at Augusta in 1991, when all his dreams were finally fulfilled.

Stalwart of Europe in the Ryder cup (above) and colourfully decked out at the US Open (opposite)

Everyone is in agreement that the 5 ft 4 inch Welshman, Ian Woosnam, is head and shoulders above most other professionals on the world's golf circuits. At the end of the 1990 season he had replaced Spaniard Seve Ballesteros as Europe's most prolific money winner with career earnings totalling over £2 million. Indeed, there were only three players — Greg Norman, Nick Faldo, and Jose Maria Olazabal — ahead of him in the world rankings table.

Yet as he entered his 15th year as a professional there was one glaring omission in his considerable achievements — the prestige of a Major championship. The nearest Woosnam had come to realising his lifetime goal is to finish joint runner-up to Curtis Strange for the 1989 US Open, and to be third behind Greg Norman in the 1986 British Open at Turnberry. Although his Ryder Cup partner Nick Faldo, and Sandy Lyle have reached the pinnacles of success in both the US Masters and British Open, Woosnam's best form always seemed to desert him when he needs it most. Everyone agreed that when he eventually managed to marry inspiration with occasion, the rest of the world would be left trailing in his wake.

In the last three years the dynamic little man with the ability to wallop a golf ball further than the big men of the game, has produced periods of sublime golf. In 1987, when he laid claim to being world Number One, he won eight times around the world, ending the year in a blaze of glory by becoming the first Briton to take the World Matchplay title, then capturing the World

Sergio Tacchini

Ian Woosnam's dream of a Major championship finally came true at Augusta in 1991

Cup for Wales with David Llewellyn. Woosnam was also the individual winner at that gathering of nations in Hawaii.

There were four more European titles in the next two seasons, then five during a wonderful 1990 which ended with him being European Number One for a second time, but with a new record prize haul of almost £675,000. Woosnam was in irresistible mood in shooting 60 in Monte Carlo, and 62 at the Scottish Open, winning by five and four strokes and being 33 under par for the eight rounds. An Open championship and a hat-trick beckoned at St Andrews, but Nick Faldo put paid to that. Woosnam did finish fourth, six strokes behind, but the flame had dimmed at the wrong time again.

Woosnam built his muscles working on the family farm at Oswestry after leaving school, and his early years in golf were equally hard labour. Born on 2nd March 1958, he turned professional at 18, but had to make three visits to the qualifying school before establishing himself on the European tour. Victory in the now defunct News of the World Under-23 matchplay confirmed his promise, but his career did not take off until three years later when he won the World Under-25 title and the Swiss Open in 1982.

Like those other diminutive Welshmen Dai Rees and Brian Huggett, Woosnam has been ideal Ryder Cup material, making his debut in 1983, and playing a key role in the European triumphs at the Belfry and Muirfield Village. Moreover, he confirmed his matchplay prowess by winning the world title for the second time at Wentworth in the autumn of 1990.

Woosnam considered that Augusta, where European players won the Masters four times between 1985 and 1990, offered him the best chance of winning a Major championship, and this belief was confirmed at Augusta in 1991 when he played beautifully to capture the US Masters ahead of Olazabal and an inspired Tom Watson. The Welshman has indeed landed.

CAREER HIGHLIGHTS

Major titles

US Masters: 1991

Other achievements

Ryder Cup: 1983-85-87-89

World Cup: 1980-82-83-84-85-87-90

(Winner team with David Llewellyn 1987

Winner Individual 1987)

Dunhill Cup: 1985-86-88-89-90

FUZZY ZOELLER

The crowds flocked in from afar to witness the engaging play of this talented entertainer. Despite continuous back problems, the inimitable 'Fuzzy' rewarded his admirers with a hugely popular US Open success in 1984.

Enjoying the atmosphere at St Nom la Breteche in 1985

He may be last in the alphabet but this fun-loving extrovert from Indiana would be first in most polls to find the galleries' favourite personality. Fuzzy — his nickname comes from the initial capitals of his full name Frank Urban Zoeller — put the smiles back into what was becoming an all too serious business during his meteoric rise to stardom in the 1980s and the crowds flocked to acclaim this hugely talented entertainer. Zoeller, born on 11th November 1951, exhibited a joie-de-vivre that was infectious as he set out to show that playing golf was as, he frequently remarked, 'better than working for a living'.

In his first full season on the US tour in 1975 he finished 146th and won just over US$7,000, but said he enjoyed spending five times as much! After winning the 1979 Masters at his first attempt, and the 1984 US Open, he was a champion clown in every sense — but one with an inner steel. Very few realised that Fuzzy was in almost

Fuzzy has achieved golfing success despite being plagued by back problems incurred from a High School injury

continuous pain from back trouble, the legacy of a basketball injury at high school. It became public knowledge when, after winning a play-off against Greg Norman for the US Open at Winged Foot, he journeyed to Shoal Creek, Alabama for the US PGA Championship. When he awoke on the morning of his first round his back had stiffened so badly he could barely move. He was rushed to hospital and stayed there for the rest of the tournament.

Within a month he was undergoing surgery for two ruptured discs and was out of golf until the following year. The mark he had already made was considerable after his first victory in the San Diego Open early in 1979 which qualified him for Augusta. This was the Masters that Ed Sneed lost as he bogeyed the last three holes to allow Tom Watson and the unfancied Zoeller to tie on an eight under 280. Fuzzy's golf had been steady rather than spectacular but in the first sudden-death play-off — the previous six had been over one or two rounds — he holed an eight foot birdie putt at the 11th, the second extra hole.

Zoeller's US Open triumph five years later owed nothing to fortune. First he beat off the challenge of Hale Irwin who had dominated when Winged Foot had caused everyone so much trouble in 1974. Then he tied with, and defeated, Norman by a commanding eight strokes in the 18-hole play-off. In a thrilling last-round finale Zoeller endeared himself to a worldwide audience by waving a white towel in mock surrender after mistakenly believing that the 40 foot putt the Australian holed on the last green was for a birdie. Zoeller was playing the 17th when Norman carved his second shot into the stands at the 18th, and had not seen him overhit the flag with his third from the dropping area. When he realised a par four would put him level, Zoeller managed it comfortably. Fuzzy took a three-stroke lead at the second in the play-off with a birdie to Norman's double-bogey, and from five ahead at the turn, won with a 67 to a 75.

Zoeller won three times in 1986, when he was also eighth in the British Open, having finished in the same position behind Watson at Troon in 1982. The nearest he came to a US PGA title was to finish runner-up to Larry Nelson in 1981.

CAREER HIGHLIGHTS

Major titles

US Masters: 1979

US Open: 1984

US Tour victories 10

Ryder Cup: 1979-83-85

Swinging through the sand at Augusta during the US Masters

The Great Rounds

A great round of golf is not simply an exercise in statistical excellence. There are other factors to consider, such as the quality of the course, the weather, the opposition, whether it be stroke or match-play, and perhaps more importantly, the occasion.

Invariably the rounds that attract most attention and are remembered long after the event are compiled in the Major championships, although the Ryder Cup and World Match-Play have also provided memorable examples. Into the latter category go the stunning performance of Faldo and Woosnam in the 1987 match between Europe and the USA at Muirfield Village, Ohio, and Jacklin's enthralling contest with Trevino at Wentworth's Burma Road. Sometimes the drama and significance of the occasion have overshadowed the actual figures on the card. Nobody would suggest that Sam Torrance was rewriting the Belfry course record in 1985, but the Scot enjoyed his finest hour at that Ryder cup climax.

The last-day domination of Gary Player and Jack Nicklaus to win the 1978 and 1986 Masters titles are among the best examples of a golfer approaching perfection when it mattered most. The closing rounds produced by Seve Ballesteros to take the 1984 and 1988 Opens were similar masterpieces.

There are those that insist that the duel in the sun between Watson and Nicklaus at Turnberry in 1977 will never be surpassed; some marvel at the onslaught unleashed by Curtis Strange at St Andrews, or Sandy Lyle (photo left) and his rescue act at the final hole of the 1988 US Masters.

Others speculate on what effect Olazabal's annihilation of Akron will have on his rivals as he sets out to be the dominant player of the 1990s. Every golf fan has his special memories. The following are a selection of mine.

US Masters 1968

Augusta

A scorecard muddle in the last round robs Roberto de Vincenzo of victory

Most golfers find fame by winning Championships. Roberto de Vicenzo and Doug Sanders share the distinction of being more famous for titles they lost rather than won. Sanders has a permanent niche in Open Championship history as the man who missed from less than three feet at the 18th and forfeited the 1970 title at St Andrews, where next day he was beaten in a play-off by Jack Nicklaus. Roberto's great mistake came after he had finished his final round in the 1968 US Masters at Augusta.

The Argentinian, the best golfer to come out of South America, and one of the most popular players on the World's circuits, had shot 65 on his 45th birthday. It was registered as a 66 because in the excitement of the moment he failed to notice that his playing partner American Tommy Aaron had incorrectly marked a par four on his card at the 17th. De Vicenzo had in fact scored a birdie 3 there and 20,000 spectators as well as 20 million television viewers had seen him do it. However, under the rules the higher score had to stand and Roberto's total of 278 was one stroke too many to put him in a play-off with another American, Bob Goalby. The prize-giving ceremony was one of the most poignant in the history of Championship golf, although there had been no guarantee that De Vicenzo would have added the Masters title to the British Open he had at last claimed nine months earlier at the Royal Liverpool club, Hoylake. That had been the crowning point of a professional career which began in 1938 and contained more than 200 victories by the time he captured the US Seniors Open in 1980.

Roberto, who was born in Buenos Aires, was already a prolific winner in South American tournaments when he first visited Britain in 1948. He was joint third behind Henry Cotton on his Open debut at Muirfield, and third again the following year behind Bobby Locke. In 1950 he shared the lead with Locke after three rounds at Troon, but finished with a 70 to the South African's 68 and was runner-up by two shots.

Roberto kept on trying, and was third on three more occasions, to Peter Thomson at Hoylake in 1956, then Kel Nagle and Tony Lema at St Andrews in 1960 and 1964. When he returned to Hoylake three years later it was 'really to see all my old friends', said the big ambling Argentinian, whose geniality had endeared him to British golf fans. They had long recognised his ability, for Roberto had won respect for his long driving and the quality of his iron play. If he had a weakness it was on the green, where he was fond of joking to others: 'I play like a motor bike — all putt-putt-putt'.

That week, the South American made few mistakes with his putter and with his customary chequered cap hiding his thinning hair, Roberto was very definitely the favourite of the galleries as he took on defending champion Nicklaus and the formidable Gary Player. A third-round 67 put him into a two-stroke lead for the last leg, and despite a 69 from Nicklaus, De Vicenzo held on to win by two strokes with a 70. At 44 years and 93 days he had at last achieved his life's ambition, 19 years after his first Open appearance. He remains the

'He has always been noted for his fair-play, self-control, self-denial and generosity of spirit... and has always shown respect for the game and the people in it.' The Bobby Jones award for distinguished sportsmanship was given to Roberto de Vicenzo in 1970

oldest Open champion this century. Roberto had won for the first time in the USA in 1951 and had six wins to his credit there when he arrived at Augusta in the spring of 1968. The first three days of that Masters provided a feast of scoring and the South American had opened with a 69 to be among the early front-runners. A follow-up 73 and 70 left him well placed for a last round charge, although few seriously believed the man who had suffered so much disappointment on the big occasion was likely to follow in the immediate footsteps of Nicklaus and Gay Brewer. The former was already the dominant figure, having taken the Masters in 1963,1965 and 1966, the latter after a play-off with Brewer and Tommy Jacobs. Brewer's turn had come in 1967.

The start of Roberto's last round signalled that this April 14 would be a memorable anniversary, for he hit his second shot at the 400 yards straight into the hole with a nine-iron for an eagle 2. A drive and long iron got him home at the long second where two putts secured a birdie 4, and another birdie followed at the 355 yards third where his pitch finished less than a foot from the flag. Four under par after three holes, and the putter had been used only three times! Much more of that and Roberto would not have to worry anymore about his shaky form on the greens.

He played the next four holes immaculately for par figures before again opening his shoulders to reach the 530 yards eighth in two shots. The birdie 4 enabled him to turn in 31. The journey round Amen Corner was not without incident, but Roberto was in no mood to let shots slip away. Although his mid-iron approach to the 10th found sand, a good recovery left him with only a four foot putt for par which he comfortably made. A more accurate iron gave him a good birdie chance at the 11th which got away, but he made up for that at the dangerous 12th where his 6-iron tee shot pitched beyond the flag then edged down 12 feet below the pin. In went the birdie putt and another followed from similar range at the 15th after he had laid up short of the water. At that stage Roberto was seven under and the Masters was in his sights. Meanwhile Goalby, who had been runner-up for the US Open in 1961 and the US PGA title the following year, was also finding birdies plentiful, as was another fellow American Bert Yancey in a 65 for 279.

Goalby, risking all over the water, was rewarded with an eagle 3 at the 15th. Amid mounting excitement Roberto, who was two holes ahead, hit a perfect wedge off a huge drive at the 17th, and left himself only a yard from the pin. Down went the putt for his sixth birdie, and now only the 420 yards uphill 18th remained.

Roberto hit a good drive at the last and selected a 4-iron for his approach. The shot was slightly pulled and he was left with an awkward little chip from which to secure the four that would probably just edge him to victory. The South American manoeuvred his ball six feet from the hole but his putt spun out for the only bogey of his birthday celebration. De Vicenzo was still rebuking himself as he entered the recording area. He knew the lapse could be crucial, for Goalby's task as he prepared to play the 17th was now clear — two pars to win. Roberto could not complain. It was his error at the 18th which had opened the door. There was nothing to do but wait and see. As he headed for a television interview his spirits rose. Goalby had three-putted the 17th to drop back to eleven under par alongside Roberto and his 65 for 277. When the American hit his drive at the 18th into trees, the galleries were at fever pitch. Goalby rose to the occasion by perfectly fading a three-wood from under the branches to the heart of the green. Two putts gave him a par four, a round of 66, and as everyone thought a tie with De Vicenzo. Whether it was the highly charged atmosphere, the distractions of the media, self-recrimination at his last hole mistake, or simply his Latin temperament that was responsible for the scorecard calamity, must remain conjecture. Despite repeated checks, Roberto did not notice Aaron's error on his scorecard. He signed for a 65 but the figures for which he alone was responsible added up to 66. Everyone knew he had taken three at the 17th, but his card was marked '4', and Roberto had signed for the higher figure. Rule 6-6(d) is quite explicit on this matter. If a competitor returns a score for any hole higher than actually taken, the score as returned shall stand. There was pandemonium when the news became generally known around the course.

Goalby, convinced he would be in a play-off, was astonished to learn he had won on such a clerical technicality. Officials scampered to and fro, pursuing every possible path around the error. An approach was even made to the ailing Bobby Jones, around whose legendary exploits the Masters concept had been founded. Arguments about the fairness of the rules in

In 1967 at Hoylake — and on his way to winning the British Open

such a case, were, he deemed, superfluous. The player is responsible for the accuracy of the hole-by-hole scores marked on his card. Roberto's four at the 17th must stand.

De Vicenzo accepted his fate with exemplary grace, giving his sympathetic audience at the prize ceremony a sheepish grin. 'Making friends is more important than making money', he said. 'But what a stupid man I am.' Goalby said later that he would much rather have been beaten in the play-off than be known as the man who took the title by default. The following year Masters officials revised their checking system, and it is now an established procedure at all Major events that the players are taken to a separate area away from outside influences. An official goes through the card, hole by hole, and a player may take as much time as he likes before signing for his scores. In 1970 Roberto won the Bobby Jones Award for distinguished sportsmanship in golf. That has probably given him more pleasure than the vast majority of the cups and medals in his trophy cabinet.

The Open 1969

Royal Lytham and St Annes

Tony Jacklin ends an 18-year drought for British golfers at the Open, and the crowd sing 'For He's a Jolly Good Fellow'.

Tony puts the 6-iron to work as he lofts the ball towards the flag

Every now and then a sportsman emerges who captures the imagination of the public. Henry Cooper, George Best, and latterly Paul Gascoigne, are among those who have plucked the heart strings of the nation and been showered with adulation and affection. In 1969 a young man from Scunthorpe, Lincolnshire became such a national sporting hero when he ended Britain's victory drought in a Major golf tournament.

To generations of golf fans accustomed to the all-conquering exploits of overseas players, Tony Jacklin was the answer to their prayers. Just 25, good-looking, with a magnetic personality, and blessed with a sublime talent for striking a golf ball, he was a champion in whom everyone could be proud. Postwar golf in Britain was dominated first by South African Bobby Locke, then Australian Peter Thomson. After him came Arnold Palmer, Gary Player and Jack Nicklaus, and for 17 successive years the famous Open claret jug went overseas.

It had been 18 years since Max Faulkner won for Britain at Royal Portrush, but in Jacklin the nation at last found a golfer who could take on and beat the World's best. The emotional scenes that greeted his Open triumph at Royal Lytham and St Annes that summer were not matched until Jacklin himself was the architect of the return of the Ryder Cup to British and European hands at the Belfry in 1985. There was scarcely a dry eye on the Lancashire links on that July day as the crowd greeted the overdue home win with a lusty rendering of 'For He's a Jolly Good Fellow'. Even the Press corps was visibly moved, greeting 'Our Tony' with a standing ovation when he was eventually released by the backslappers to relate his version of the day's events. How Jacklin rose from lorry driver's son to become the first of Europe's superstars, and subsequently the inspiration for today's multimillion golf circuit, remains more compelling than any single round he ever played at Lytham.

For the record, he made the necessary good start with a 68, followed with two solid rounds of 70, then closed with a 72 for a total of 280 to hold off New Zealand's Bob Charles by two strokes. Any doubts about Jacklin's victory were dispelled the moment he struck a majestic drive to split the fairway at the 72nd hole which left him a comfortable 140 yards shot to the flag.

Jacklin had started life as a £3 a week apprentice in the local steelworks and at 17 had left home to become an assistant to Bill Shankland at the Potters Bar club in North London. Shankland was a former Australian Rugby League international who had twice finished third in the British Open. He was a hard taskmaster, and in his book *The Price of Success* Tony described his time there as 'like doing the National Service that I never had to do. It made me, and I could not have had a better grounding.'

It was not long before the teenage Jacklin's tournament ambitions became incompatible with his employment as an assistant performing all the mundane tasks that keep a club shop in good order. With the financial backing of some of the club's wealthier members, he parted company with Shankland and set out to seek fame and fortune as a touring professional. The young Jacklin was quickly at home in the electric atmosphere of big-time golf. He had finished 30th in his first Open at Lytham in 1963 although he had to borrow £5 to get back to his digs in Potters Bar. The £2,700 that Tony won in 1966 looks paltry in comparison with today's mega-prize funds but he used it wisely, ploughing it back into the business by investing in a winter campaign in

Unleashing a powerful drive down the fairway

Two putts from around 12 feet at the 18th...

Australia. While 'Down Under' he got a lucky break. Neil Coles' aversion to air travel had led him to turn down an invitation to the 1967 US Masters. It was passed to Jacklin who had just won his first international cap in the World Cup in Japan. Jacklin was inspired by Augusta and the American golf scene and resolved to return as quickly as possible. It was a decision that was to give him the confidence and determination to become a supreme champion.

The previous year he had won his first British tournament, the Blaxnit in Belfast, and married his first wife Vivienne shortly afterwards. They headed West to chase the crock of gold at the end of the American rainbow. Within eight weeks of joining the US tour in 1968, Jacklin had become the first British golfer to win there for almost 50 years. His victory at Jacksonville, where he also won in 1972, was the springboard for the momentous events at Lytham and in Minnesota the following year. When Jacklin

set out to tackle the overseas monopoly of the Open at Lytham, he had become an imaginative golfer of the highest quality. Most importantly he also had just the right blend of arrogance and belief in his own ability. The British fans certainly believed in him as Tony made the perfect start, holing from six yards on the first green for a birdie. By the sixth he was four under par, nice insurance for the assault on Lytham's unrelenting inward half. He came in with a 68 for a share of second place, two shots behind Charles who had opened smartly with a new course record of 66. That was trumped by Ireland's Christy O'Connor with a 65 on the second day which moved him into second place, with Jacklin just three shots off the lead.

The hours that the teenage Jacklin had spent in bunker practice paid off in the third round as he beat par for the third day running. The galleries groaned as time and again Tony's approach shots drifted into sand. They need not have worried. Jacklin

...and it's all over as Tony acknowledges the applause of an appreciative audience

never failed to get out and down in two strokes, sinking a string of putts from six to ten feet to protect his figures.

His 70 put him on a five under par 208, with Charles who had slipped to a third day 75 sharing second place with O'Connor on 210. Just behind were the 1967 winner Roberto de Vicenzo and Peter Thomson, the five times champion. Jack Nicklaus, who had begun poorly, had fought his way back into the reckoning and had put himself in striking distance on 213. Two shots ahead and with the expectation of a nation on his shoulders, Jacklin faced a long night and a long wait the next day until his starting time. Tony was paired with Charles and quickly had the measure of the left-hander. The New Zealander dropped a shot at the first and by the fifth tee was five strokes adrift as Jacklin sank birdie putts of five and twelve yards on

Sharing his triumph with his wife

the third and fourth greens. When they reached the far end of the course, Jacklin had a four shot lead over the field, with the wily old fox De Vicenzo his nearest rival after getting out in 33. Charles and O'Connor were five back and the rest struggling to match the card against the blustery breeze that had sprung up to increase the problems going home. Charles cut his leeway with birdies at the 10th and 13th, Jacklin dropping a shot at the latter through an underhit pitch, but there were still three strokes between them after they negotiated the 16th. The rest had fallen away so surely, the crowd felt, the Open was at last about to come home.

Three putts from Jacklin and a bogey at the 17th raised a ripple of apprehension. The 18th was a dangerous hole with bunkers to catch anything but a long straight drive, and scrubland to snare the slice or push. Jacklin's answer was to unleash his finest drive of the week. It zoomed straight as an arrow down the fairway. A gentle 7-iron, followed by two putts from 12 feet and it was all over. Britain had its own Open champion, and when Jacklin came back from the USA with their Open title the following June, leading from start to finish for a seven-stroke triumph, it also had its first golf Superstar.

A memorable Ryder Cup match at Royal Birkdale in 1969 and an outward 29 in his Open title defence at St Andrews the following July added further lustre to the Jacklin halo. He was in the thick of the action at the next two Opens, and Britain had no finer golf ambassador. He returned to Europe and laid the foundations of the modern European tour by triggering massive commercial interest in the professional tournament arena. Crowds flocked to the game, spurred by dramatically increased television coverage which in turn had new sponsors rushing to secure nationwide exposure, and paying handsomely for the privilege. The golf boom was under way and Jacklin was the toast of Britain. Later there was a price to pay and once Jacklin's material ambitions had been realised he lost enthusiasm for the nomadic life and razzmatazz, until the Ryder Cup provided him with a second crusade. But that's another saga.

World Matchplay 1972

Wentworth

A see-saw battle between Lee Trevino and Tony Jacklin captivates the crowded galleries at Wentworth.

Lee Trevino, thunders a drive towards the 5th green as his supporters look on anxiously

When Tony Jacklin followed his Open victory in 1969 by capturing the US Open Championship the following June, he had the golf world at his feet. For the next three years he chased further fame and fortune, driven on by his ambitions and his adoring fans. 'I want to be a millionaire and I want to win all the world's Championships', he declared after Lytham. Wherever he played the crowds flocked to watch England's new golf hero. Superagent Mark McCormack was taking care of the Jacklin finances, all Tony had to do was keep playing the brand of golf that had made him the best of British, and the first to win the US title since Ted Ray in

1920. Unfortunately for Jacklin, another young man with exceptional gifts and the same burning desires was emerging from the wrong side of the tracks in Texas, and their paths were to cross repeatedly in the early 1970s. Lee Trevino, a former US Marine from Dallas, had emerged from his own spartan upbringing to win the 1968 US Open and was fast becoming Mr Personality-Plus of the American golfing scene.

Jacklin and Trevino first pitted their skills against each other in the famous 1969 Ryder Cup tie at Royal Birkdale where two years later 'Supermex' was to win the first of his British Open titles. Jacklin, as Open champion, beat Jack Nicklaus in the morning singles on the last day and then halved with him in the afternoon to secure the tie. However, in the previous afternoon fourballs, Tony and Neil Coles ended a titanic struggle with Trevino and Miller Barber on level terms to keep the match square at 8-8. From then on, wherever Jacklin turned Trevino always seemed to be around to thwart him, whether it was matchplay or strokeplay. Even though Jacklin made a spirited defence of his Open title at St Andrews in 1970, where he played the first nine holes of his first round in 29, Trevino finished third behind Jack Nicklaus, one stroke ahead of Tony.

The next year Trevino was unstoppable as he won the US Open, Canadian Open and British Open all within five weeks, and was always in command at Birkdale, pushing Jacklin down to third place. In that September's Ryder Cup in St Louis, they met again. Trevino won four of the first five holes of their singles and though Jacklin rallied he lost on the last green. When the Open Championship returned to Muirfield in 1972 Jacklin, suffered the cruellest of setbacks when Trevino chipped in at the 71st hole and went on to snatch a second successive title away from playing partner Jacklin. If the two previous Opens had been disappointing, Muirfield was a shattering personal blow to Jacklin who once again finished third. All week he had played great golf, but for two days he had seen Trevino sink outrageous putts and shots from off the green. In the third round Jacklin had 67, but Trevino holed a bunker shot at the 16th, then chipped in at the last to close with five successive birdies and a 66. All these heartbreaking experiences were still fresh in Tony's mind when fate flung these two masters together yet again in the 1972 World Matchplay Championship at Wentworth. The event had begun in 1964 and no British golfer had won in the first eight years, although Neil Coles had reached the first final against Arnold Palmer. Nevertheless, expectations of another Jacklin home win were high when he crushed American Grier Jones in his opening match and qualified to meet Trevino in the semi-final. For sponsors Piccadilly it was the box office sensation.

In an epic battle for supremacy, Jacklin matched Trevino shot for shot, and this long-iron recovery from out of the rough proved no exception

Could Jacklin gain revenge? Would the Mexican magician cast his spell once again? Scheduled for 36 holes over the Burma Road, West Course it went every inch of the full distance, and many still regard it as the greatest encounter in the history of this long running autumn spectacular.

A huge crowd lined the first fairway when Jacklin and Trevino stepped onto the first tee with Tony determined to try a new approach. He was concerned that his concentration might be upset by Trevino's constant on-course chatter and had told Lee that he would prefer not to talk. Trevino's response was to exclaim: 'You don't have to. All you have to do is listen.' One up to Trevino before a shot was struck in anger. At lunch Jacklin was four down, to an opponent who had gone round in 67 and had won the 17th and 18th. At that time the par for the West Course was 74 with the first and 15th both just qualifying as par fives.

That afternoon Jacklin played the finest golf of his career, scoring 63, with nine birdies and an eagle, and still lost. It was heartbreak time again for Tony, but in truth he had no cause for self-recrimination . He played magnificently and so did Trevino. Those lucky enough to be there were treated to an afternoon of wondrous wizardry. Jacklin's revival began at the fourth where he struck a 5-iron approach from short of the cross-ditch only five feet from a flag tucked behind the guardian bunker. The eagle cut his deficit to three, and Jacklin got another one back at the short fifth where his 6-iron never left the flag and finished barely two feet from the hole. Trevino now knew he had a fight on his hands, and made his first mistake by overhitting his pitch to the sixth. Jacklin, who was only four feet away in two, was conceded his birdie putt and was only one down at this stage.

A perfectly placed long-iron set up another winning birdie for Jacklin at the eighth where his 6-iron over the pond left him a straightforward six foot putt. He was level, and amazingly one ahead with yet another birdie 3 at the ninth. Here an immaculate drive and 5-iron second, put him five feet away and he made no mistake to turn in 29. An eagle, five birdies and three pars had transformed the match and Trevino's 35 for the same stretch looked pawky in comparison.

A spot of the rough stuff for Trevino as well, but nothing would deny the mercurial Texan that day

Yet Trevino was level after a birdie at the short 10th, where Jacklin ran through the green and could do nothing about his rival's shot a yard from the pin. But he struck back immediately at the 11th, regaining the lead with a putt of 13 feet for his birdie 3, only to have the smile wiped from his face when Trevino eagled the long 12th for the second time that day. Jacklin's birdie 4 from a chip to four feet was to no avail as Lee ran down his 18 foot putt after getting home in two perfectly struck strokes. Jacklin saved the 13th by chipping within a foot of the hole for his par 4 and the next three holes were halved, the 15th in birdie fours. Both missed birdie chances at the 16th from the 20 foot range, so they were still level as they prepared for Wentworth's demanding finish. Neither could reach the 555 yards 17th in two, but both played pitch shots of the highest calibre. Trevino went first, landing his ball six feet away. Jacklin got inside him by hitting the flag. Both holed for birdies, so it was on to the 495 yards last. Both hit good drives, but Jacklin was the shorter and closer to the trees screening the right side of the fairway. Jacklin needed a 3-wood to get home and had to fade it to hit the target. It kept going straight and finished in the light rough left of the green, leaving him an awkward pitch . Trevino's left-to-right shot did not present him with any difficulty. Such strokes are his stock-in-trade. He found the heart of the green, and when Jacklin, who had pitched well to around ten feet, saw his birdie putt slip wide, Trevino was left with two putts for the match, both a mere eight feet from the hole.

He took both to win by one hole and leave Jacklin wondering just what he had to do to rid himself of the man who had tormented him for three years. Jacklin was eleven under par for the afternoon, had shot two eagles and 12 birdies in the day, and still Trevino was triumphant. Jacklin's only consolation was that he had forced him to produce figures of almost equal quality.

Trevino had responded to Jacklin's outward change by covering the inward half in a five under par 32 for a day's total of 134. It contained two eagles and 14 birdies. Jacklin had been stunned after his Muirfield experience, but he was more philosophical after Wentworth. 'Losing to Lee in the Matchplay was my own fault', he said. 'I was so sure I was going to beat him, but I missed the green with my three-wood at the last hole and that mistake cost me the match. I shot 63 but it ended with a fatal error.'

The Open 1977

Turnberry

Watson and Nicklaus re-enact the Gunfight at the OK Corral during that long hot summer of 1977.

The summer of 1977 was long and hot, especially on the west coast of Scotland. When the crowds poured into Turnberry for that year's Open Championship, they were greeted with a golden setting for a contest that has since been called 'The great duel in the sun'.

No two players have so dominated a Championship as Tom Watson and Jack Nicklaus on the Ailsa course that July, when only the brilliance of the perpetual sunshine matched their strokeplay. For four days they rivalled each other shot for shot, leaving the rest of the world far behind in their fight for supremacy. It ended with Watson, the sharpshooter from Kansas City, victor by one stroke with an all-time record total of 268, and the Golden Bear ten shots ahead of third-man Hubert Green.

It was the second time that season that Watson and Nicklaus had collided in pursuit of a major title. Americans were still recounting their head-to-head clash for the Masters, where Watson had produced a last day 67 to hold off the charging Nicklaus, who closed with a 66. It was all so reminiscent of the latter's own challenge to the dominance of Arnold Palmer over a decade earlier. Watson had proved at Augusta that he had the courage and conviction to succeed to the Nicklaus crown.

Turnberry established him as a great champion, and Nicklaus acknowledged it. The heatwave had virtually eliminated the rough; what grass there was had ripened like summer corn, and the fairways were

The crowds flocked to Turnberry in 1977 for the first ever Open to be held there — and what an occasion it proved to be

firm and fast. So were the greens, and only the perfectly struck approaches held. It was links golf at its traditional best, and the ability to 'feel' distance and manufacture shots was more important than a yardage chart. Significantly, although he was approaching his 48th birthday, Peter Thomson, who had won five Open titles in similar conditions, finished 13th, ahead of all the Europeans except Horton.

Watson and Nicklaus both began with rounds of 68 and 70 and so were partners in the third round, a mouth-watering prospect for the sun-basking galleries whose number fully justified the decision to place Turnberry on the Open rota for the first time. The crowds had had their appetite whetted on the second day by an astonishing 63 from American Mark Hayes, still the lowest score in the history of the Championship. Hayes clipped 13 strokes off his first round offering, and by putting himself on the heels of the leaders provided an extra spur to the Watson-Nicklaus rivalry. That intensified on the Saturday when over 30,000 spectators and millions more via television watched agog as both shot 65 to post 54-hole totals of 203. Only Ben Crenshaw was within reach, his third round 66 leaving him three shots behind. Watson and Nicklaus were thus paired again for the final round, and soon after dawn all roads to Turnberry were

Watson plays a great recovery shot from the bunker during the final round... and edges ever nearer to Nicklaus

jammed with traffic heading for the showdown between the great titans.

The pressure on Watson was enormous even though he had already proved his worth with victory in the 1975 Open at Carnoustie, and a few months earlier with his first Masters success. Remember Nicklaus at that point had already won 14 Majors and had compiled a formidable Open record, having only twice finished outside the top six in his 15 previous appearances. In addition to winning in 1966 and 1970 he had been second four times, and third on three more occasions. When he began the fourth round with two birdies, going three ahead because Watson pulled his mid-iron approach wide of the second green, another Golden Bear triumph looked odds on. Surely no one could give Nicklaus that start. But that day an inspired Watson could, and when Crenshaw and the rest quickly fell out of the reckoning, Tom started his surge.

After saving himself at the third by getting up and down from a greenside bunker, Watson threw down the gauntlet with his first birdie at the fifth, attacking the flag with a 5-iron, and holing from 15 feet. Watson bunkered his 3-wood shot to the elevated green at the short sixth, but got his recovery within a yard to save par, and then outhit Nicklaus at the 528 yards seventh, hitting two driver shots on to the green and two-putting for the birdie that put him only one stroke behind. This was gripping stuff, and those spectators not already caught up in the excitement abandoned the earlier players. In their eagerness to get close to the action, they held up play several times as Watson and Nicklaus neared the spectacular Bruce's Castle ninth hole.

It took some time to complete the eighth, where Watson wiped out the early Nicklaus lead with his third birdie in four holes. Again it was engineeered by a superb 5-iron shot to some 25 feet, and Watson's putter did the trick before the club and its master were forced to take an unscheduled rest. Both players had to wait on the beach while extra crowd marshals were summoned to clear their way to the pinnacle above the rocks which serves as the tee to the ninth. The crowd was six deep on either side of the fairway when Watson was eventually able to hit, and he pulled his drive badly into rough. He found a good enough lie to get a long-iron at his ball, but was unable to find the green some 230 yards away, and had to accept his second bogey of the stretch. He was out in 34 against a 33 from Nicklaus and one behind again. No one else was within eight shots of Watson.

It had now become an epic matchplay encounter in which every stroke was crucial. Both made their fours at the 10th, and also their pars at the short 11th, the Maidens,

Nicklaus and Watson take time out on the beach before ascending to the 9th tee promontory, 'on the edge of a gaunt granite cliff that tumbles down behind you to a rock-strewn toussled sea'

although Watson bunkered his 6-iron shot. Then Nicklaus went two ahead with his third birdie at the 12th and once again seemed to have the decisive edge. When they turned at right angles towards the clubhouse and the long homeward run, few gave much for Watson's chances. The 13th, a gentle left-to-right dog-leg with an elusive green, was made for Nicklaus, and surely his power would count in the tough finishing stretch.Yet Nicklaus did not make the expected birdie at the 13th, where it was

Nicklaus warmly congratulates Watson at the 18th...

Watson who hit the more accurate pitch to the elevated green and holed from ten feet. Now the gap was again one stroke, and still so after regulation fours at the 14th. The next was to reinforce Watson's growing belief that this would be his day after all.

Turnberry's final short hole can require anything from a driver to a 7-iron depending on the wind, with danger on all sides. A steep hollow lies short right of the green to trap anything not boldly struck. Deep bunkers skirt the left flank of the putting surface to trap any shot that overdoes the safety line. Watson put himself in no-man's-land, equidistant between the two no-go areas, but short of the green and some 65 feet from the flag. With Nicklaus contemplating a makeable birdie chance, Watson's misjudged 4-iron looked like being a costly mistake. As so often happens, the roles were dramatically reversed. Watson holed with a perfectly weighted putt and Nicklaus missed. All square with three to play.

The burn at the 16th was negotiated without alarm, and both hit good drives up the funnel of the 500 yards 17th. Watson went first for the green, striking a 3-iron with a precision Nicklaus could not match. Nicklaus selected a 4-iron, which he hit solidly, but pushed a fraction. He was left with a testing chip from a fluffy lie which he played well to within five feet of the hole, and more or less on the same line as Watson who had an eagle chance from 25 feet. Watson left his first putt hole-side and tapped in for his birdie, but Nicklaus after stalking his putt for an eternity, misread it and so was behind for the first time in two days. Watson drilled his 1-iron at the last far past the bunkers guarding the dog-leg, and with Nicklaus pushing his drive into the base of a gorse bush had at least one hand on the famous trophy. Before Nicklaus could assess his next task, his rival had hit a peach of a 7-iron just four feet from the 18th pin. Somehow Nicklaus thrashed his ball on to the front edge of the green and with a magnificent gesture of defiance, sank a putt of fully 30 feet for the birdie that gave him the chance of a play-off. Watson would have none of it. He calmly stroked his ball into the hole to bring down the curtain on perhaps the greatest of all Opens. His second 65 made it the lowest last two rounds, as well as the lowest winning aggregate. Nicklaus closed with a 66 and his 269 remains the lowest total by any Open runner-up.

Turnberry had made its Open bow, but it was Watson and Nicklaus who received the standing ovation as arms around each other they left the arena. 'I gave it my best shot but you beat it', said Nicklaus in Watson's ear. Third man Hubert Green provided another memorable postscript. 'Two gods of golf played their own game', he remarked. 'I won the tournament for the mortals.'

...and Tom salutes the crowd after a famous victory

US Masters 1978

Augusta

The evergreen South African Gary Player becomes the oldest winner in Masters history.

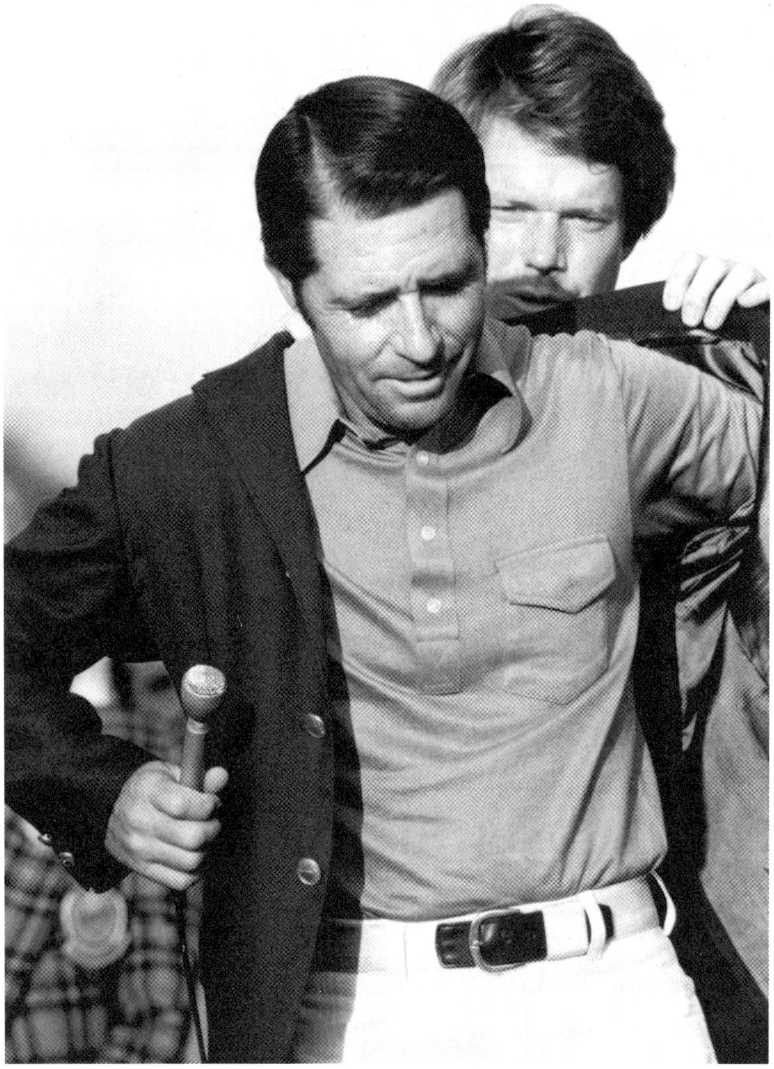

Next stop vaudeville! Gary looks the part as he accepts the Green Jacket from Tom Watson

Augusta, they say, is a young man's course. The hills are hard to climb, and the greens are even harder to putt on. Definitely no place for any golfer burdened with the increasing frailties of middle age. The history of the Masters is littered with those who have become spectacular casualties in the autumn of their careers — just ask Tom Weiskopf. Four times a runner-up, 'Long Tom' took 13 shots to hole out at the short 12th in the first round of the 1980 event, and he was a mere stripling of 38!

When Gary Player reported for the first Major of the 1978 season he too looked to be a waning star, although one for whom there was universal respect . The little South African had eight Major titles to his credit, stretching over a gruelling 20 years of worldwide campaigning, and had twice been Masters champion. The first occasion had been back in 1961 when he became the first overseas winner, taking the title from Arnold Palmer. The second was in 1974, the year he also won his third and last British Open. Although Player had continued to be successful at home, particularly in the South African Open, he had not won on the US tour since. The 1974 season had also witnessed his 100th professional victory.

In 1976 Player was elected an honorary member of the US PGA, and elder statesmanship was beginning to beckon with his appointment as first captain, then president of the South African PGA. Player was well into his 43rd year when he returned to the familiar surroundings of the Georgia plantation. By the end of the week he had once again confounded convention, and also revealed his best-kept secret.

The South African's opening rounds were unremarkable, but a pair of regulation 72s saw him comfortably past the hurdle of the halfway cut. On the third day he took advantage, like the rest of the field, of ideal scoring opportunities to produce a 69, and give promise of a highly respectable finish.

'It's a cinch, boss'. On the 18th and Gary's going for gold — or in this case, green!

Easing the ball towards the final hole...

Defending champion Tom Watson was everyone's favourite, the memory of his magnificent last day duel with Nicklaus the previous April still fresh in their minds. Watson had not disappointed, producing two rounds of 68 after a somewhat shaky opening 73, to stand seven under par, four ahead of Player but still three strokes back of leader Hubert Green. The reigning US Open champion had catapulted himself to the top with a 65 on Saturday for a 54 hole score of 206. The stage was therefore set for a last round battle between the current US Open and Masters champions, with another American Rod Funseth bracketed with Watson on 209, largely on the strength of a highly creditable second round 66.

How Player overturned this equation remains one of the miracles of the Masters which has never ceased to provide a surfeit of drama. All through his career he had shown the capacity to achieve the impossible, no cause being irreparably lost. He is revered in Britain for his exploits in the World Matchplay Championship at Wentworth where his record of five victories is still unsurpassed. The first was in 1965 when he came back from six down at lunch and seven behind after 19 holes to defeat Tony Lema at the 37th in the semi-final, and went on to beat Peter Thomson. Player's escape from impending doom was not approached in achievement until Sandy Lyle recovered a six-hole halfway deficit to beat Nick Faldo 17 years later. At Augusta in 1978, Player again displayed his never-say-die spirit when he began the last round seven strokes behind Green, and beat him, Watson and Funseth by one shot to become the oldest winner.

Maybe it was the youthful exuberance of his partner that provided Player with his spark. Severiano Ballesteros was celebrating his 21st birthday that Sunday morning and was in high spirits. The Spaniard had won at Greensboro' the week before when he came from five strokes back after 54 holes to defeat his playing partner Lanny Wadkins, then the US PGA champion, by one stroke. Seve had just been given an invitation to compete in that summer's US PGA Championship and had also been offered his card for the US tour. Neither did Ballesteros hide his admiration for the determination and tenacity that had made Player a legend in the game. He had already exhibited a good measure of both qualities in emulating the South African by showing that 'a foreigner' could succeed in the USA if he had the talent and resolution.

In addition to a 'sympatico' companion, Player also had another priceless asset — his superb fitness. All those years of self-discipline, diet and exercise had made him fitter than most men half his age. He was feeling good, the sun was shining, and he was playing well.

Player's early golf in that sensational final round was not startling, although there were two birdies in the first four holes. At the second he showed he had lost none of his powers of recovery from sand, by nursing a greenside bunker recovery to within a foot of the hole for his birdie 4. Then at the short fourth, which always plays less than its nominated 220 yards, he was home with a 5-iron and holed from 30 feet for a two. A stroke was lost at the seventh, where he drove into the trees and again found greenside sand. This time Player did not save himself, missing a putt of six feet. A birdie chance of eight feet also escaped at the long eighth, after which he was still where he began, seven shots behind Green who had only recently started his last lap. At the ninth, Player birdied again, his 7-iron approach from a downhill lie leaving him an uphill putt of 12 feet. He turned in 34. A 25 foot putt fell for his fourth birdie of the day at the 10th, but he was thankful to walk off the 11th green with a par 4 after missing the target across the water flanking the green. A cleverly played chip that hugged the contours of the slippery surface left his ball inches from the flag. It was at the short 12th, where the tee shot has to be struck with such precision across Rae's Creek, that Player realised he could set a target the rest might find difficult to overcome. His 7-iron over the water floated down 15 feet from the hole, and another birdie was on his card. Two majestic strokes to the 13th gave Player an eagle chance from similar distance, but that was not to be, and he departed Amen Corner content with a fourth birdie.

The South African was now within two shots of the lead and news of his exploits electrified the galleries rushing to monitor his progress. The 14th did not fall to his onslaught, but only narrowly survived, for Player missed from around eight feet. His next stroke of real merit was the 3-wood he struck unerringly over the water to the heart of the 15th green to set up his seventh birdie. He still had to get down in two putts from nearly 20 yards, but he duly accomplished that far from easy task to give himself a share of the lead. A watery grave always threatens at the 16th, but Player gained another huge fillip from a 5-iron which covered the flag, leaving him a putt of some four yards. To the delight of the onlookers he holed it, and pinned his concentration on the two closing par fours. The 17th yielded nought, but at the last Player and Ballesteros were cheered almost the whole way to the green, after the South African had hit a near perfect approach to the final target. When he rolled in a 15 footer for yet another birdie, the crowd were almost delirious with delight. Player had birdied seven of the last ten holes for a total of 277, but had a lengthy wait to see whether it would be good enough for a third Masters triumph. One by

...and 'gotcha!' A final birdie seals the greatest win of his career

one the contenders failed, Watson and Funseth shooting 69 for 278, and then only Green was left. At the last he faced a three foot putt to force a play-off but missed, and Player's victory was assured. He described his golf that day as the finest he had ever played, and subsequent events bore out that judgment. Player remained in the same sublime form to win the Houston Open and Tournament of Champions in the next fortnight to make it three US wins in a row. The Masters statistics also required amendment. Player's 17-year winning span from 1961-78 was the longest in Masters history, and his 64 was the lowest last round by a champion. In addition, he was almost certainly the oldest winner since the inception of the event in 1934. But precisely how old? Player had one last surprise as he donned the coveted Green Jacket. He declared he was 42 years and 5 months, and that the reference books that all along had revealed his birth date as 1 November 1936 had been wrong!

At the end, a magnanimous Ballesteros congratulates the new champion. It had been a long wait for Gary Player, but well worth it

THE OPEN 1984

ST ANDREWS

Ballesteros' game plan is too much for Langer and Co at the Auld Grey Toon.

They came to St Andrews in their thousands from all parts of the globe that July of 1984. An unprecedented army of almost 190,000 poured into the 'Auld Grey Toon' on Scotland's east coast to witness the 113th Open Golf Championship. They came to honour Jack Nicklaus, awarded an honorary doctorate by the local University, and they came to see if Tom Watson could become one of the immortals by being only the second man in history to win six Opens. Harry Vardon, the supreme stylist who gave his name to the grip that is still the one most commonly used to wield a golf club, gained his six victories between 1896 and 1914.

Watson, who first succeeded across the Tay estuary at Carnoustie in 1975, had the chance to win his six in the remarkably short span of only ten years. He could also emulate Australia's Peter Thomson, the only other 20th century golfer to perform an Open hat-trick. They also came to celebrate the 23rd running of the world's premier festival at the traditional home of golf, and to discover whether the Road Hole really was the dreaded graveyard they had been led to believe in the past.

After four days of exhilarating competition they had the answer as the young man who had done more than any other to put European golf on a par with the American game in the 1980s, combined with the 17th to wreck the record-breaking dreams of the Kansas City six-shooter. For Seve Ballesteros, St Andrews 1984 was more than a triumph of strategy, concentration and determination, as he defeated Watson and Germany's Bernhard Langer by two strokes. It was also the culmination of a pilgrimage that had begun 20 years previously on the sandy shores of another bay where golf is played with just as much intensity. As a seven year old Ballesteros learnt to play golf on the beach near his home at Pedrena, across the water from the

The 1984 Open trophy — and Seve wanted it so badly

seaport of Santander in northern Spain. He used pebbles for golf balls and sticks for clubs, until his elder brother Manuel gave him an old 3-iron. Seve marked out his golf course on the wide sands below his farmhouse home and then became a caddy at the Royal Pedrena club where his uncle Ramon Sota was the professional.

A hundred years earlier the young lads of St Andrews might have done much the same along the Eden estuary before graduating to the links where the game has been played in one form or another since the 16th century. In 1978 Seve's game had not been mature enough to cope with the subtleties of the Old Course and he had finished 17th behind Nicklaus. Six years on he had already become Open champion, and twice winner of the US Masters, and though his early form had been indifferent that season, he was clearly a man for the big occasion. Ballesteros was determined not to again become a victim of the pot bunkers that had punished him so severely on his previous visit. The main plank of his game plan was to avoid them at all costs. To that end he resolved to drive on the left-hand side, the opposite of the accepted way to unlock the secrets of St Andrews. He would happily accept a more testing second shot as long as it was above ground.

Looking for distance off the 16th tee

The Spaniard was so successful with this ploy that he had to play only two sand shots that warm and sunny week, both out of the infamous 17th Road bunker during a second round 68. That put him in a share of second place at the halfway stage alongside Nick Faldo and a revitalised Lee Trevino. The trio were three behind the surprise pacemaker Ian Baker-Finch of Australia, who had opened with rounds of 68 and 66. During the latter he had lost a ball at the 10th, but escaped penalty when it was established a boy had 'snaffled' it as a souvenir. Watson and Langer were in the group on a five under par 139, but both made significant moves on the third day, the American shooting a 66 that sent him soaring to a tie for the 54 holes lead with Baker-Finch on an eleven under par 205. Faldo and Trevino both faded, but not Ballesteros. He had a 70 to be two behind on 207, although like Watson he had once again fallen foul of the 17th. The American had taken five and six there on the first two days. At the third attempt he had made his par, finding the tortuous green with the 2-iron that had served him so well in the previous year's win at Birkdale. Ballesteros had bogeyed the hole in each round and promised, 'If I make a par there in the final round I will win. If I don't I will come back on Monday and try again!' Everyone had been expecting the double-barrelled Australian to crack sooner or later under the pressure, and he quickly disappeared from the equation at the start of the last round where he partnered Watson in the final match. A pitch into the Swilcan Burn unhinged Baker-Finch at the first, and by the sixth he had dropped four strokes and was heading for a 79. Watson on the other hand was in prime position to achieve his goal of a sixth Open victory and his fifth in Scotland. The two Europeans, Ballesteros and Langer, were just ahead, both two shots lead, then went ahead when Ballesteros misjudged his tee shot and came up well short of the 11th green. No sooner had Watson gone into the lead than he lost it, driving into a gorse bush at the 12th and being forced to drop out under penalty. A birdie from four yards put him ahead again, only for Seve to level with a 15 foot birdie at the long 14th where once again he had avoided the Beardies string of bunkers by driving far left. Ballesteros and Watson were still level at 11 under after they parred the

behind, and very soon Langer was dropping stokes and allowing the title to develop into a battle between the two players generally acclaimed the World's best.

Ballesteros began with four pars, then birdied the long fifth to move to ten under and alongside Watson who had three putted the fourth. Another birdie at the short eighth sent the Spaniard to the turn in 34 and one ahead of Watson, whose putter had produced nothing of note in an outward 37 The tension rose rapidly over the next few holes as Watson birdied the 10th to share the 15th and 16th . Ahead lay the 461 yards of the fiendish Road Hole. It is probably the most famous golf hole in the world and certainly the one that has caused most controversy and consternation over the years. The cavernous bunker eating into the left side of the green was dubbed the 'Sands of Nakajima' after the Japanese golfer Tsuneyuki Nakajima had putted into it with his third stroke in the third round of the 1978 Open, and taken four shots to get out. The road beyond the green is part of the hole which stretches all the way to the stone

Seve's second shot at the infamous 460 yards par 4 17th — known as the Road Hole. This brilliant 6-iron from out of the rough proved to be a championship winning shot

On the 18th green, and a 15 ft putt heads for the hole (right)... and in she goes! (below)

No way back for poor Tom. Against the wall at the 17th (left), and despite an excellent chip and run onto the green, he fails the eagle attempt. There's no stopping Seve now (below)

boundary wall and there is nothing to prevent an overhit ball rolling down the little shelf of the green into this area. Having survived the drive over the corner of the out-of-bounds Old Course Hotel, where once there were railway sheds, the safest route is to aim the second shot at the large apron, front right of the green, and hope to get down in two more. This is where the more masochistic spectators assemble, and there were plenty that afternoon among the record crowd of 39,755. Ballesteros hit a big drive, but too far left, and his ball bounded into the rough. There looked to be no way he could make the four that would pile the pressure on Watson just behind. With the Road bunker between him and the flag Seve's moment of truth had arrived. He smashed a 6-iron into the long grass and struck the shot of the Championship as his ball soared 200 yards to land on the green. He two-putted for his four, delighted at having conquered the monster. Watson's drive at the 17th was perfect, but he then made the error that decided this Open, and will haunt him whenever he contemplates what might have been at the mecca of the game. With around 190 yards to go he selected the 2-iron which had provided him with his par 3 the previous day. He aimed for the large apron, hoping to draw the ball gently up the crest of the green to within a comfortable distance of the flag. Fatally, he pushed the shot and it whistled through the green to finish almost up against the wall. Despite an excellent chip and run, Watson was doomed to the bogey that put him one behind with only the 18th left. He had barely realised his plight when a huge roar up ahead greeted a last green birdie from Ballesteros after he had wedged 15 feet from the pin. The Spaniard punched the air in ecstacy. He had conquered Watson, the rest of the world, the Road Hole and the Old Course with a round of 69 and a record aggregate of 276... unless the American could eagle the last to tie.

With a last act of defiance Watson carefully paced out the 90 yards he had left to the final flag, but it was a forlorn hope, and his dreams collapsed with the pitch that was too firmly struck. Ballesteros had joined the elite who have won an Open at the home of golf, and there to witness his moment of glory was his mother Carmen, who had never doubted he would be the World's best when she had watched over him from her kitchen window as he played golf on the sands all those years ago. This time she was there to shed tears of joy.

Ryder Cup 1985

The Belfry

Sam Torrance defeats Andy North to help Europe triumph again after a barren run lasting 28 years.

Way, Torrance and Woosnam have a European knees-up on a day of celebration

The afternoon of 15 September 1985 will go down in history as the day European golf began its golden era. When shortly after 4 pm Scotland's Sam Torrance stood with arms aloft in the centre of the Belfry's 18th green, he signalled not only the end of 28 years of American domination of the Ryder Cup, but also that the gap in talent had firmly closed.

Torrance was not the only man shedding tears that summer Sunday after sinking the birdie putt that gave him personal victory over Andy North, the US Open champion, and simultaneously clinched Europe's first victory over the USA since Lindrick in 1957. Most of the many thousands who crammed into the West Midlands complex on that final day had lumps in the throat and moist eyes as they saluted the heroic deeds of the European team led by Tony Jacklin. From the inspirational Seve Ballesteros to the unheralded Jose Rivero — one of the captain's personal choices — they had played their hearts out. The best that the USA could muster had been beaten 'fair and square' as the margin of $16\frac{1}{2}$–$11\frac{1}{2}$ amply demonstrated. The sight of the emotional Torrance, putter pointing to the heavens, became a symbol of the supremacy Europe had waited so long to enjoy. It is still the most widely recognised photograph from that remarkable week which culminated, as though by some celestial design, with triumph being clinched at the amphitheatre of the Belfry's spectacular 18th.

The match might easily have been settled 'out in the country' and out of sight of most of the throng, when Howard Clark stood simultaneously over a four foot putt to beat Mark O'Meara at the 17th. Fortunately for posterity, and most of the photographers who had already made their choice of denouement, the Yorkshireman missed. Happily, Clark went on to achieve one of his side's seven singles wins, fully justifying Jacklin's decision to cram his strength into the middle of his line up for that last day of high drama. It was on the rock of Ballesteros, Lyle, Langer, Torrance, Clark and Way that Lee Trevino's USA team was broken, with Manuel Pinero and Jose Maria Canizares scoring the additional victories that put the icing on the cake.

Jacklin's Ryder Cup captaincy had begun with defeat in the 1983 match in Florida, but the outcome was in doubt until the final putt, and only a point separated the teams. European confidence that they could regain the trophy they had last won 28 years previously was therefore sky high, even after a disappointing start. The Americans won the first morning's foursomes by 3–1, Europe's only winners being Ballesteros and Pinero who accounted for Curtis Strange and O'Meara. Torrance and Clark, who were later to play such a prominent part in the hour of victory, were well beaten by Craig Stadler and Hal Sutton, and also lost in the afternoon, although round in 67, to Raymond Floyd and Lanny Wadkins in the fourballs. However, the Spaniards won again, Way and Ian Woosnam brought in another point, and the half that Langer and Canizares obtained left Europe priding themselves on their recovery to be $3\frac{1}{2}$–$4\frac{1}{2}$ behind. Torrance and Clark found their form in the second round of fourballs on Saturday morning, three birdies in a row from the 15th giving them a 2 and 1 win over Tom Kite and North, whom fate later decreed would be the Scot's singles opponent. Half an hour later came the turning point of the whole contest, a mistake by Stadler, the 1982 Masters champion. He and Strange had been two up with two to play against Langer and Lyle and looked set for the win that would keep the Americans a point ahead. Yet Lyle holed a 25 foot eagle putt to win the 17th and Stadler missed a two foot putt for the match at the last. The psychological boost to the European team was enormous. They had

A regal salute to the crowds. Sam was on the top of his form that week at the Belfry

Sam aglow after sinking the historic putt that brought the Ryder cup back to Europe

halved a match they should have lost and with that nervous Stadler nudge went a lead the Americans never regained. Ballesteros and Pinero descended on the shattered Stadler and new partner Sutton in the afternoon foursomes, ruthlessly despatching them 5 and 4; then Rivero and Canizares, who had been held in reserve, walloped Kite and Calvin Peete by 7 and 5 after going out in 33 to the Americans' 40. When Langer and Ken Brown made up for the sole European defeat of Way and Woosnam, Jacklin's men had a 9–7 advantage, and needed just $5^1/_2$ pts from the 12 Sunday singles. The atmosphere in the European camp that evening was one of quiet confidence that they had the measure of Trevino's side. Jacklin, his first lieutenant Bernard Gallacher, and Ballesteros had earlier discussed tactics for the morrow, reasoning correctly that Trevino would have to gamble and put his strength at the top of the order in the hope of quickly recovering the American deficit. Trevino led off with the formidable matchplay trio of Wadkins, Stadler, and Floyd, followed by Kite. Jacklin put Ballesteros at number four, followed by Open Champion Lyle, Masters champion Langer, and the battle-hardened Sam Torrance and Howard Clark.

When the pairings were revealed, Jacklin knew he had found the soft underbelly of the American side, which was now confronted by Europe's fiercest five. Europe took 4½ points from those five encounters. Almost 30,000 poured into the Belfry for the climax and the atmosphere was electric as each of the Europeans was given a thunderous ovation when he stepped on to the first tee. Jacklin saw each man off, and then kept tabs on each match as the excitement mounted. Pinero and Way were the first European winners, trumping Trevino's gamble by accounting for Wadkins and Floyd, but Woosnam went down to Stadler, and elsewhere things were not going quite as expected.

Ballesteros was three down after 13 to Kite, and although Langer was always in command of Sutton, Lyle and Clark were only one ahead, and Torrance was three down after ten to North. Down at the bottom of the order the news was even worse. The recovery that Ballesteros launched to rescue himself proved crucial. All week he had been Europe's inspiration, producing his finest strokes when they were most needed. Once again he did not disappoint his supporters. A swinging 50 foot putt to birdie the short 14th, and one of six yards on the long 15th for a four cut his leeway to one hole. Then he overpowered Kite at the 575 yards 17th, getting home in two whereas the American could not. Another birdie 4 put the Spaniard on level terms and he stayed that way to give Europe just the boost they needed at a crucial time. Within minutes Lyle had pulled away from Peter Jacobsen, Langer had routed Sutton, and the spotlight swung onto Torrance and Clark who were vying for the victory that would take Europe to the winning post of 5½ points. Torrance had fallen behind to a pair of birdies from the lofty North at the fourth and fifth, but when he went into water at three successive holes around the turn his supporters, who included his parents Bob and June, groaned aloud. He had got back the short seventh where North was bunkered, but after salvaging a half in bogeys at the eighth, put his approach into the lake at the ninth to turn two behind. Then he misjudged his pitch over the pond at the 10th and again encountered a surfeit of water to fall three behind. He looked done for, but Torrance is a bonny fighter, and a cast iron par at the 11th where North missed the green, and another win at the 15th, where the American was in a fairway ditch, cut his deficit to one hole. At the 17th he was level, pitching from thick rough to within six feet of the flag and sinking the putt for his first birdie. When the news was flashed onto the giant scoreboard across the lake from the 18th grandstands, the reaction was ecstatic. Seconds later, to gasps of amazement, his golf ball was seen bounding towards that arm of the Belfry's trademark lake that fronts the final green. It came to rest not more than 20 yards from the water, a hit of such power and precision that it was guaranteed to demoralise the toughest of opponents. That massive 300 yards blow which left him only a 9-iron to the flag, certainly stunned North. Striving for something similar, the American pulled his ball into the lake. Torrance had only to hit the green to be sure of beating an opponent who needed four strokes to get there compared to his two.

Now it was just a question of who holed out first, Torrance or Clark who was crouched over his birdie putt a hole behind. To Torrance went the honour of the coup de grace, and the right to tell his grandchildren the tale of the putt that won back the Ryder Cup. Rightly, Sam will never forget that Sunday afternoon, and neither will all of us who had waited a lifetime to share his great moment of jubilation.

Torrance gives captain Tony Jacklin a boost as the celebrations begin

US Masters 1986

Augusta

'I love golf, and I can still play a bit.' A final-round 66 enables Jack Nicklaus to rewrite the record books... and keep his promise.

In April 1986, Jack Nicklaus won the Masters for a sixth time. Twice before he had donned the Green Jacket with better winning scores and by bigger margins, and others had done so too. But nobody had won the title at the age of 46. Not for the first time in his phenomenal career, Nicklaus had the obituary writers squirming with embarrassment, even though on his arrival at Augusta he had half agreed with their predictions by declaring rather wistfully, 'I am in the December of my career.' Yet it remains true to this day that no one in the history of the sport has been able to transform his game so successfully on the big occasion, and if Augusta 1986 does prove his Major swansong, there could be no more fitting a setting than the luscious greens of Georgia's golfing cathedral.

Against the likes of Norman, Ballesteros, Watson, Kite, Price and Stewart, the pundits decided that week that the ageing Golden Bear had little chance. His early 1986 form had been miserable by any standard. In seven preliminary tournaments he had only once been in the top 40 and had won barely enough to keep his caddy in hamburgers. This time he had brought eldest son Jackie to be his fairway companion. How was he to know that the father they said was a spent force was still capable of producing the finest pressure round in Masters history? That it should be played on the last day of the 50th running of the Masters by the man who alone had surpassed the achievements of its founder gave it a special significance.

Until the advent of Seve Ballesteros, Nicklaus had been the youngest Masters champion in 1963. Now 23 years later he was about to replace Gary Player as the oldest. The instrument of his mastery was a last round of 65. Opening rounds of 74 and 71 did not inspire great optimism among the Nicklaus clan or his army of supporters congregating among the Augusta pines. The expected favourites Norman and Ballesteros were well ahead, and even a third round 69 which lifted Nicklaus to two under after 54 holes still left him four shots behind leader Norman. Yet Nicklaus was once again inspired by the atmosphere of Augusta. His tee-to-green golf had improved considerably each day and he told Jack Jnr he was sure he had a chance, if only he could hole some birdie putts. 'If I shoot 65 I can win', he predicted to second son Steve, 'and a 66 might be good enough to get a tie.' After seven holes of the final lap neither target looked within his compass. Nothing was happening. His solitary success had been a birdie at the second from a three yards putt, soon to be cancelled by three putts at the short fourth. At the 180 yards sixth Nicklaus missed a short putt for another birdie, and if he was to make rapid progress it had to be started soon. Ahead lay the long uphill slog of the eighth and Nicklaus simply had to get home in two and take his birdie chance. Who knows — he might even get the bonus of an eagle.

He wound himself up for a big drive and crashed it 300 yards, into the pines trees flanking the right of the fairway. When Nicklaus reached his ball he found his way forward blocked by trees, although some six yards ahead of him was a six-foot wide

Jack's working up a head of steam on the second day

opening between two large trunks. The sensible shot was to punch an iron through the gap to leave himself a comfortable pitch to the green. Nicklaus decided to go for the green with a 3-wood. Lady Luck always piays a major role in golf, and this time she smiled broadly on the Golden Bear. His ball whistled between the gap in the trees, but not the one he intended to bisect. It went through a 12-inch hole between the right-hand pine and another large conifer, and finished just off the edge of the green. The birdie got away but the 3-wood escapade set the adrenalin flowing.

Another big drive at the ninth, this time splitting the fairway, gave Nicklaus another

'Who said there were few bunkers at Augusta?' Jack retrieves the situation with a delicate chip

Jack and Jack Jr in isolation on the deceptively wide fairways at Augusta

birdie chance he did not let slip. He wedged some 12 feet above the hole and rolled in the putt to turn in 35. From then on there was an air of marvellous certainty about his putting. He used the club only 13 times on an inward half that for sustained brilliance was to rank at least the equal of Gary Player's in 1978. Both came home in 30, the difference being that Nicklaus had five birdies and an eagle, partially offset by a bogey at the 12th, whereas Player had six birdies and no blemishes. At the 10th Nicklaus stepped up his momentum by hitting a towering 4-iron to the middle of the green and holing from 25 feet. He completed a birdie hat-trick at the next where his 8-iron approach came down 20 feet from the flag, and that putt too disappeared. He was then three under for the day, five under overall and just two strokes adrift of Norman and Ballesteros. Nicklaus was now obviously very much in contention, but a sixth Masters still looked a very tall order, especially when he slipped at the dangerous par three 12th. A slightly pulled 7-iron over Rae's Creek put him on the back fringe of the narrow green from where he chipped some seven feet from the hole. The par putt slid by and Nicklaus looked to have made a very costly error. The crowd were soon hollering again when after another huge drive at the 13th Nicklaus hit the par 5 in two and walked off with another birdie. Norman and Ballesteros had at first been puzzled by the din up ahead, but when they saw the name of Nicklaus following theirs on the leader boards all the excitement became clear.

The Bear was on the rampage. His tee shot at the 15th was perfect — long and straight — and his 4-iron to the green plummeted down 12 feet from the flag. The new Macgregor putter, which had been performing such miracles, stroked the ball home for an eagle that was greeted with a roar no one could misinterpret. The galleries were still buzzing after Nicklaus struck another inspired shot off the 16th tee. His 5-iron to the final short hole left his ball only a yard from the flag. In his mood that was another certain birdie and the crowds responded with a cacophony that forced those players immediately behind to back off their shots in alarm. Among them was Ballesteros, about to play his approach to the 15th. When the Spaniard did eventually settle, striving for the birdie 4 that would keep him two ahead of Nicklaus, he hit a dreadful 4-iron which dived left into the water fronting the green. With that smothered stroke, betraying the pressure of the moment, went Seve's hopes of a third Masters. Meanwhile, Nicklaus went to eight under by securing his two at the 16th, and was hellbent on adding the one further birdie that would secure his target 65. He overdid his draw off the 17th tee, his ball running wide of the fairway on to a hard patch of ground between two pine trees. This time it was not the trunks that were inhibiting, but an overhanging branch that prevented him hitting an orthodox pitch. Nicklaus improvised beautifully, punching a low wedge under the rim which then climbed and came down ten feet from the flag, grabbing the green with its side-spin. The putt up the slope never looked like missing the cup, and for the first time Nicklaus was in the lead.

It seemed as though the whole of America was behind Nicklaus as he fired his final drive to the centre of the 18th fairway, and struck his 5-iron second to the safe middle area of the last green. When he laid his long approach putt to within inches of the hole, Augusta erupted. Nicklaus had played the last 10 holes in seven under par, and shot 65 for a nine under 279. Jack and Jack Junior left the green, arms around each other, and waited to see if the young men could catch the old Master.

Ballesteros had already perished in his watery grave, while Price and Watson were consigned to the minor places. Only Kite and Norman had realistic chances to overhaul Nicklaus. The former's last hope disappeared when his birdie putt at the last ran over the hole, but the Australian had battled to be level at nine under par when he reached the 18th tee. A play-off between the Bear and the Great White Shark, his close friend and near-neighbour loomed as Norman's ball landed plumb centre of the final fairway. A birdie 3 to win and a 4 to tie. The Australian got neither, hitting a stroke that was as destructive as the one that undermined Ballesteros at the 15th. He pushed it so wide of the green that a bogey was an achievement, and he finished tied second with Kite, one behind.When Bernhard Langer, the 1985 champion, performed the traditional task of helping Nicklaus into the familiar Green Jacket it was one of the most emotional moments anywhere in the game. 'May be this is the ideal time to say goodbye, but I'm not quitting', Jack said afterwards. 'I love golf and I can still play a bit.'

That is why no one dare risk writing him off again, not even now that he is officially a Senior. If anyone is to become the first over-50 to capture one of the World's four great Championships, it is odds on that Nicklaus will be that man.

And wasn't that two-week diet of carrots worthwhile in the end, Jack?

Ryder Cup 1987

Muirfield Village

The Faldo-Woosnam double act — the 'long and the short' — inspire the Europeans to their first victory on US soil.

If regaining the Ryder Cup in 1985 signalled the renaissance of the European game, then retaining it with the first victory on American soil two years later, broadcast to all and sundry that it had reached magnificent maturity. The quality of golf produced by Tony Jacklin's team at Muirfield Village in 1987 was of a standard never before achieved on a collective basis. Even skipper Jacklin was left breathless by the spectacular shot-making of that European side which reached its zenith in the second series of fourballs on the second afternoon. That excellence was expressed most graphically by Nick Faldo and Ian Woosnam, whose furious onslaught destroyed Tom Kite and Curtis Strange, and enabled the Anglo-Welsh partnership to emerge unbeaten from their four matches. In spotlighting the two Britons one must never forget that the three and a half points Faldo and Woosnam gained must always be viewed in the context of a team effort. They inspired others by their brilliance, but they were also inspired by others of their own side. Two other combinations — Seve Ballesteros and Jose Maria Olazabal, and Bernhard Langer with Sandy Lyle — also produced consistent world-class golf in those foursomes and fourball engagements .

So emphatic was the superiority of the 'Super Six' that the Europeans rejoiced in a lead of 10–5 going into the final day's singles. That the final scoreline in that historic triumph should be 15–13 to Europe speaks volumes for the glorious uncertainty of matchplay, and the strength of the American resolve not to surrender their unbeaten home record that had existed since 1927. But lose it they did, and with their defeat went the notion of American supremacy in golf that had begun to look increasingly fragile following the success of Ballesteros, Langer and Lyle on the US tour.

Faldo had been badly out of form during the 1985 match at the Belfry and had lost the only match he played on the first two days, and his singles as well. However, he had just won the Open championship after reconstructing his swing under the guidance of the Florida based British coach David Leadbetter. His final round at Scotland's Muirfield was a masterpiece of accuracy and concentration, made up of an amazing 18 successive pars.

Jacklin reasoned that the long — Faldo is 6 ft 3 inches — and the short — Woosnam just makes 5 ft 6 inches — could be a devastating mixture of acumen and aggression. He sent them out as his third pair in the first series of foursomes against Lanny Wadkins and Larry Mize who had won the Masters that year after a play-off with Greg Norman and Ballesteros. When Faldo and Woosnam lost the first three holes and turned for home four down they looked destined to be an embarrassing flop. The news from elsewhere was also grim as the temperature soared into the eighties. Up ahead, Howard Clark and Sam Torrance were three down to Strange and Kite, and second pair Langer and Ken Brown were trailing by two. Even anchormen Ballesteros and Olazabal were struggling two behind in the bottom match to Larry Nelson and Payne Stewart. Nelson had beaten the

Spaniard four times when they first clashed at the Greenbrier in 1979 and had won all nine of his Ryder Cup matches. However, the recovery that Faldo and Woosnam launched after taking 40 strokes for the first nine holes was to transform Europe's fortunes, and by that evening Jacklin and his team knew they had the spirit and the ability to achieve something extra special.

Faldo began the fightback by hitting his 3-iron approach to the 10th just five feet from the pin, and Woosnam tapped home the winning birdie. When Wadkins found sand at the short 12th, the deficit was down to two. Another Wadkins mistake at the 14th, where he drove into the stream, cost the Americans another hole, Then Woosnam hit the shot of the match at the uphill 490 yards 15th. A piercing one-iron found the middle of the green and a two-putt birdie made it all square. Wadkins and Mize scrambled a half at the 16th, but fell apart over the last two holes which the British pair took with par fours to claim a stunning victory. They had won six of the last nine holes which they covered in 34 strokes and when the Spaniards won on the last green, Europe were level at 2–2.

Just what effect the Faldo-Woosnam revival had on their team-mates became clear during that afternoon's first round of fourballs. Clark and Torrance had given way to Gordon Brand Jr and Jose Rivero, while Langer had been reunited with his old partner Lyle. Faldo and Woosnam were again at number three, followed by Ballesteros and Olazabal. For the first time in the history of the event, Europe completed a 4–0 'whitewash'. The USA had previously done it six times. An eagle and two birdies in the space of four holes from the 11th took Faldo and Woosnam to a 2 and 1 win over Hal Sutton and Dan Pohl, and by nightfall Europe had a handsome 6–2 lead. The

English pragmatism combined with Welsh wizardry proved too much for the Americans. They say that a touch of the old ultra-violet always works wonders!

Faldo leads the Charge of the Light Brigade on the second day, as a vital putt goes down at the 14th

Britons had a tougher fight next morning, ending level with Sutton and Mize in the second series of foursomes, but that was only a lull before the storm they unleased on the unsuspecting Kite and Strange after lunch. Europe led $8^1/_2$–$3^1/_2$ going into that second session of fourballs, and it was vital to preserve that five point advantage for Sunday's closing singles. This time Jacklin put his aces at the top of the order. Their response was to produce one of the greatest ever exhibitions of fourball play.

Kite and Strange had won two of their three previous games, and that morning had responded to the urgings of American captain Jack Nicklaus with a convincing win over Brand Jr and Rivero. They looked a tough proposition, even for the in-form Europeans, and showed their mettle by parring the first five holes. But by that stage the match was effectively over, for Faldo and Woosnam opened up with a barrage of five successive birdies between them, scoring 3-3-3-2-4 against the Americans' 4-4-4-3-5. Woosie began the blitz by hitting his approach to the first a mere two feet from the flag. Faldo hit second shots of similar quality and holed from four feet on the next two greens. Then up popped Woosnam again to send down a 12 foot birdie putt at the short fourth, before Faldo comfortably made his short range birdie putt at the long fifth. That was sensational golf by any standard, and more was to follow. Although Strange did birdie the sixth to get one back and the Americans shared the seventh in birdie fours, another two from Faldo at the eighth sent the Europeans back into a five holes lead at the turn which they reached in just 29 strokes, seven under par. Woosnam had the crowds roaring again when he hit a long-iron a yard from the 10th flag for his side's eighth birdie and then it was only a question of the size of their triumph. American birdies at the 11th and 12th enabled them to avoid an unwelcome entry in the record books, but the Europeans were in no mood to allow any chance of escape. Faldo put them five down with as many to play with birdie number nine from five yards at the 13th, and Woosnam put them out of their misery with the tenth at the 14th for a resounding 5 and 4 victory. Woosnam exclaimed, 'We showed that we now have a world class team. We got so excited that we never thought about being tired. We just concentrated on making as many birdies as we could, and to prove we could win over here.' Skipper Jacklin, for whom Langer and Lyle also came up trumps for a 2–2 scoreline, added, 'I never thought I would live to see the standard of play we saw that day.'

Faldo and Woosnam had played a monumental part in taking Europe to their five-point lead after two days, and it was time for others to dredge deep into their reservoirs of determination. Together they had picked Europe off the floor on that first morning, and they had both produced majestic golf at the same time to send shudders of apprehension through the American side. Each was asked to produce one more herculean effort, Woosnam against the massive Andy Bean at the head of the singles order, and Faldo against Mark Calcavecchia. Although both matches went to the last green, both lost and Europe had to look elsewhere for their last day heroes. They found them in Howard Clark and Eamonn Darcy, Sam Torrance and Bernhard Langer, and finally the mighty Ballesteros. He beat Strange, sinking the Cup winning putt at the 17th. Then the celebrations began.

It's congratulations all round as Faldo and Woosnam come from behind to defeat Wadkins and Mize — and start the European steamroller

Dunhill Cup 1987

St Andrews

The 'Old Lady' is tamed as Curtis Strange makes a whirlwind 62 that leaves the experts mesmerised.

There have been many rounds of 62 in professional golf during the last 25 years, but none that caused as much consternation as that to which Curtis Strange put his signature one October Sunday morning in 1987. If there was any lingering doubt that the modern stars play a game that our forefathers would not begin to recognise, it was swept away that day by the Virginian. He caught the 'Old Lady' course at her most vulnerable, and left her humiliated.

It was bad enough that Australia's Rodger Davis had brought her to her knees 36 hours earlier by scoring a 63. But a 62 ... that was a positively indecent assault that left old timers rubbing their eyes and wondering where it would all end. For centuries her would-be conquerors had been kept at bay by natural defences and a magical mystique perpetuated by those with a vested interest in maintaining her dignity. Not for nothing do her gnarled weather-beaten caddies talk knowingly of the perils of the Beardies, the Coffins and Hell bunker to a never-ending stream of wide-eyed pilgrims to the cradle of the game. When at the same time the wind howls in from St Andrews Bay and even the seagulls are grounded, the audience remains discreetly respectful. They have read about or seen on television the profusion of pot bunkers waiting to snare the unwary, the huge double greens where it is not uncommon to take four putts, and the wind can batter your face all the way out, and be against all the way home. One can almost see the ghosts of Old Tom and Young Tom Morris and the Kirkaldy brothers roaming the links where golf has been played for over 400 years.

St Andrews is the home of golf and the seat of the Royal and Ancient, but above all, as the locals will never tire of telling you, it is where history has always been made. It was made in 1873 when the first Open Championship was held at St Andrews, and in 1960 when the Centenary Open was staged on the Old Course. It has gone on making history as in 1970 and 1978 when Nicklaus became the first to win two Opens there since James Braid, and again in 1990 when Nick Faldo became the first Briton to win there for 51 years. But none of the 24 Open champions at St Andrews made history like Curtis did on that balmy October morning. The American had been drawn to play Greg Norman in the curtain-raiser to the Dunhill Cup final, and though there was more than a passing interest in the outcome of the third place play-off between the USA and Australia, the real business of the day was the meeting of the 'auld enemy' to decide the destiny of the trophy and a kingly £200,000 winning team prize. A final between England and Scotland, spiced by a captains' clash between Sandy Lyle and Nick Faldo, promised a very tasty main dish. It did not disappoint as Faldo shot 66 to win by three shots and lead Engiand to a 2–1 victory, but the hors d'oeuvres completely stole the show. Strange had already won the Canadian Open that season and his success in the World Series had been his third victory on the US circuit, taking him to the head of the American money list which he had first topped in 1985. Yet his form in the early rounds of the medal matchplay event that week had not been exceptional. He had scored 71 to beat Constantino Rocca and lead the USA to a 3–0 victory over Italy, then 68 to defeat Norio Suzuki by two strokes in the second round tie with Japan. A 73 in the semi-final against Scotland had not threatened to match Sam Torrance, who had a 69 as the home team won 3–0. Davis had been the most impressive of the Australian trio, his 63 in the flat calm of Friday afternoon against Dan Halldorson of Canada although there was a difference of £20,000 between third and fourth place money for each team, and the two captains were playing for approximately £6,500.

Strange began promisingly with a solid drive to the widest fairway in golf and wedged over the Swilcan Burn some six yards from the first flag. He sank the putt, then after missing from slightly shorter range on the next green, wedged some seven feet from the third hole, and ran down that one for his second birdie to jump into an

Curtis tees off on his way to an astonishing round of 62. The Old Course had never seen anything like it throughout its 400-year history

being acclaimed as a new Old course record.

Neither Strange nor Norman had any premonition that one of them was about to produce a round of seismic proportions although it was a sunny autumn day with a gentle sea breeze of just enough strength to ruffle the flags, and there was no better setting for a pleasant game of golf. There was more pride than purse at stake, early two-stroke lead over the flaxen-haired Australian. The American's play over the next three holes remained admirably professional, his one mistake costing him nothing to the card. That came at the 564 yards fifth where, helped by the breeze, Strange was able to get home with a 5-wood second shot. He only just made it however, and from more than 25 yards took three

putts. At the fourth, a drive favouring the left side, and a good 4-iron was followed by two putts for par from around 30 feet.

It was Strange's stunning golf around the Loop , that stretch of six holes on the edge of the Eden estuary, that transformed his round. Both of St Andrews' two short holes are in the run from the seventh to the 12th, the others being short par fours, all less than 380 yards. Scores of 18 against the par of 22 have on occasion been recorded. Strange reduced the Loop to just 16 strokes, birdying every hole with a display of pitching and putting of the highest quality. The spark that set off this display of fireworks was his sand-wedge, nipped off the fairway, to the seventh green. His ball finished just five inches from the hole. At the eighth, his 5-iron tee shot left him 16 feet from the flag, and the birdie was clinically taken.

In the 1970 Open, Tony Jacklin holed his pitch at the ninth, which measures 356

yards, for an eagle 2 to get out in 29. Strange could not quite manage that, but his 9-iron to that ninth flag was accurate enough, and a 12 foot putt for his birdie 3 put him out in 31. The 10th, named after the legendary Bobby Jones, fell as well when he wedged only four feet from the target, and the short llth, where Jones had tore up his card in exasperation in the 1921 Open, yielded his seventh birdie of the day when Strange struck a 7-iron shot high over the huge Strath bunker guarding the flag. He holed from 15 feet, then from eight good paces on the 12th where again he took driver from the tee, and left himself an easy wedge. So far excellent. There were eight birdies on his card, his driving had been nigh on perfect for he had not found a single bunker, and his putting had been inspired. But the breeze was now in his face, and the hardest holes were yet to come.

Strange chose the tight line at the difficult 13th and dodged the Coffins, a fiendish nest of bunkers in which a golfer really is dead! He was able to get home with a 2-iron, although still almost 30 yards from the pin. It was a testing moment, but he laid his long approach putt stiff and happily walked off with a par 4. He settled for par again at the 14th, where a drive, 3-iron for position, then a 5-iron got him safely home. The 15th fell to a birdie putt of 16 feet which put Strange nine under the card and he eased past thre 16th with a regulation four, although his 7-iron approach had flirted with Wig bunker. Now just the dreaded Road Hole 17th remained to be conquered before he reached the relative sanctuary of the broad 18th.

Strange played the 17th in copybook fashion, his drive being perfectly positioned, and his approach shot with a 4-iron finding the front right half of the narrow green. That still left him a long approach putt, but from 24 yards Strange got close enough to make the second for a highly satisfactory par 4 a formality. When he stepped on to the 18th tee, the gallery had quadrupled as if by magic. It was four or five deep all the way to the green behind which the stands had filled in anticipation. 'I knew exactly what I had to do', said Strange after pulling out his driver for the 16th and last time. The shot was long and straight, leaving the American a pitch of around 100 yards over the Valley of Sin. That too was a gem, right over the top of the flag to settle 14 feet away. The gods of golf smiled sweetly on Curtis and his 27th putt of a day he will always remember, rolled unerringly into the cup. Strange could not have been given a warmer reception if he had won the Open. He had made history with the round of a lifetime, and that was something no amount of money could buy.

Heading for home on the 18th tee... and a place in the record books

THE OPEN 1988

ROYAL LYTHAM AND ST ANNES

The 'car park champion' Ballesteros drives his adversaries to the wall with a last round 65... and later reflects on the greatest round of his life.

He's done it! Gripping stuff as Seve celebrates

When Severiano Ballesteros won his second Open title at St Andrews, it was inconceivable that he would have to wait another four years to again put his name on one of the four Major championships. Winner of the US Masters in 1980 and 1983, then indisputably Master at the home of golf the following summer, the Spaniard was on top of the World, seemingly about to make further progress towards becoming the dominant international figure in the game.

Instead he had suffered continuous frustration, notably at Augusta, where he had been runner-up to Bernhard Langer in 1985, then seen his hopes again thwarted the following year when Jack Nicklaus at the age of 46, shot a stupendous 65 to take the Masters for a sixth time. Seve had of course contributed to his own downfall, surrendering a two-stroke lead by hitting his second shot into the water at the 15th, just as Nicklaus was on the point of birdying the 16th. The Spaniard had made a pawky defence of his Open title at Royal St George's, one of his least favourite courses, and although he blazed to a closing 64 to equal the last round record the next year at Turnberry, he had ended eight shots behind new champion Greg Norman. In 1987 he never came to grips with the problems of Muirfield and placed 51st behind Nick Faldo. Earlier he had promised a revival in finishing third in both the Masters and US Open. Seve's relatively poor showing in the Majors was something of a mystery because in 1985 he had won five times in Europe, and also in the USA, while the following season he had collected six victories. After a modest 1987 season after which he dropped from first to sixth in the European rankings there were those who were beginning to wonder whether he could win another Championship when he arrived at Royal Lytham for the 117th Open in 1988.

Ballesteros provided the answer in his

Whipping up a storm on Royal Lytham's fairways. Seve was in an uncompromising mood that week

own inimitable style with his greatest Championship round so far, a sizzling 65 for a two-stroke triumph over Zimbabwe's Nick Price. With that one round Seve removed all doubts that he was back where he belonged, on top of the golfing world. His confidence had come flooding back on the same Lancashire links where he had first become a true champion, and at 22 the youngest Open winner of the Century. That was in 1979 when he beat off the might of the American invasion to first win the title by three strokes from Jack Nicklaus and Ben Crenshaw. Other Americans including Hale Irwin had been less than complimentary about the Spaniard's golf, dubbing him 'the car park champion' because of the way he played the 16th in the final round. Seve had made a birdie there after finding his ball underneath a parked car, and being awarded a free lift.

Ballesteros was to make them pay dearly for that jibe, especially as it was founded on a total misconception. He had deliberately hit his drive into that area of sparse rough

'I spy with my little eye, something beginning with...'

which had been trodden down by spectators. It was some 20 yards off the fairway but it needed a huge hit of around 290 yards to find a position which gave him by far the best aproach to a green only 65 yards away. There had been no cars there the previous days, but on the last the R and A had utilised the area for overspill parking, never dreaming that anyone would deliberately play the hole that way. But then Ballesteros had been flouting convention all that week, aiming for those downtrodden patches of light rough, way out beyond the fairway ropes. It was a strategy he had formulated in practice with his mentor, the great South American Roberto de Vicenzo, and was the key to his victory. Those who complained that he hit the ball 'all over the place' missed the point by as much as Seve missed some fairways. Nine years later, though, such a strategy would have courted disaster and the Spaniard adopted a different game plan. This time he would keep to the straight and narrow, and concentrate on avoiding a lusher Lytham's bunkers, of which there are said to be one for every day of the year.

The rivalry between European and American golfers had reached fever pitch the previous September when Tony Jacklin had led his Ryder Cup team to a brilliant first win on US soil. Jacklin was to unwittingly stoke up further fires when he predicted another European victory at Lytham where no American professional had won the Open. Bobby Jones had been champion in the first Lytham Open of 1926, but had then been an amateur. The atmosphere was nicely on the boil when the field set off for the first round with a boisterous wind at their backs. The first nine holes at Lytham are the shortest in Championship golf, and all head in the same direction. It is where the basis of a good round must be laid, for the journey home into and diagonally against the wind is one of the longest, and toughest. The early front-runners were seeing their cards ripped apart by the wind when Ballesteros set out on his first round by birdying the first three holes with immaculate golf. He also birdied the sixth and seventh, both par fives, to turn in only 30 shots and leap straight to the top of the leader board. The Spaniard had to take his medicine coming home, notably at the 14th where he put a long-iron second shot into bushes and had to take a penalty stroke, and at the 18th where he pushed his drive on the wind into the scrubland on the right of the hole and again dropped out under penalty. Nevertheless, he had set out his stall with a 67 and was clearly the man to beat. When Curtis Strange, the US Open champion, took 79 and an ailing Jack

Looking tense yet purposeful, Seve prepares for his charge on the final day, with Zimbabwan Nick Price keeping close tabs on his progress

Nicklaus returned 75, Jacklin seemed to have made a telling point! Price made his move with a 67 on the second day to take over the lead, and kept it for a further 24 hours after torrential rain forced Saturday's scheduled third round to be postponed. For the first time the Open had to go to a Monday finish and when Price had 69 on Sunday he awoke to a two-stroke lead over Ballesteros and Nick Faldo, who was making a sterling title defence. A third Open champion, Scotland's Sandy Lyle, was a shot further back.

Superstition has always had a place in the Spaniard's scintillating career, and he came out for the last leg in the same navy blue ensemble he had worn in 1979, relieved only by his white shirt and shoes.

The first Ballesteros thrust came at the long seventh. Price played his second shot first and hit it only six feet from the flag for an obvious eagle chance. The Spaniard then hit a glorious long-iron to ten feet and holed for his own eagle. Price duly made his to stay one shot ahead, but by the 11th was one behind as an inspired Ballesteros birdied the eighth from 12 feet, the 10th after driving within a few yards of the green, then the 11th with a pitch that finished within five feet of the flag. When he mis-clubbed to the short 12th they were level once more, and it took another piece of Spanish magic to keep him that way at the 13th where Price almost holed his approach. Ballesteros sank a six yard putt for a matching birdie 3. Price, who had narrowly failed to beat Tom Watson at Troon in 1982, refused to back away over the remaining holes, and it was not until the 16th that Ballesteros regained the lead. Once again this par 4, where fortune favours the brave, proved decisive. Seve's three shots this time were inch-perfect, a one-iron to the heart of the fairway, then a 9-iron which deposited his ball less than a foot from the target. He was now one stroke ahead with two holes to play, and despite a brave four at the 17th the gallant Price was still a stroke adrift when the pair reached the final tee.

He had seen off Lyle and Faldo, the latter's three putts on the seventh green where both he and Ballesteros had eagled, consigning the Englishman to a distant third.

But he could not shake off the Spaniard. It was at the 18th that Seve showed the world his greatness after he had slightly pulled his second shot into the rough back left of the green. The man whose wizardry around the greens has become a by-word in the game, conjured up a majestic stroke to thwart the Zimbabwean once again. His perfectly weighted chip floated out of the grass and ran slowly down the green to the hole, flicking over the rim and finishing inches away. His par 4 was secure and Price was faced with a putt of almost 50 feet to snatch a tie. It was beyond him, and so was the next one, but that was of no consequence for he still had four shots in hand over Faldo. It had been a marvellous battle and Price with rounds of 70-67-69-69 had done everything expected of a front-runner. Unfortunately for him, he had come face to face with a golfing genius in full flower. 'It is only once every 50 years that you see a round like that', said Ballesteros after his 65, a score that only Tom Watson among Open champions had previously managed on the last day.

Chipping beautifully from off the green at the 18th (opposite) to leave himself with a 6 ft putt for victory, and (below) it's 'smile for the birdie' as the trophy is his

US Masters 1988

Augusta

A marvellous final-hole bunker shot caps a memorable week for Scotsman Sandy Lyle.

The 1980's witnessed a bountiful supply of golf shots that made history. The chip in from the side of the 17th at Pebble Beach that sent Tom Watson to US Open victory over Jack Nicklaus in 1982; the marvellous 2-iron that Watson struck to the 18th at Royal Birkdale to capture the 1983 Open; and the 6-iron that Seve Ballesteros fashioned from the Road Hole rough at St Andrews to win his second Open the following year. Then there was the bunker shot that Bob Tway sank at the final hole of the 1986 US PGA Championship at Inverness, Ohio to snatch victory from Greg Norman, and the 45 yards chip and run that gained Larry Mize an unlikely 1987 Masters title against Norman.

Yet when one considers stupendous strokes that earned fame for their perpetrators, there is one that stands foremost among all others. It was produced by Britain's Sandy Lyle at the final hole of the final round at Augusta in 1988, and has gone on attracting superlatives ever since. The 7-iron stroke that Lyle played from the fairway bunker at the 18th was truly great because of the circumstances under which it was executed. Not only did he have to birdie that last hole to win the Masters that April Sunday, he had to play the shot to perfection to give himself the chance of a sinkable putt for the three that would, at a stroke, so to speak, transform failure into glory. Lyle did everything required, picking his ball cleanly off the sand, and sending it whistling to the heart of the green 150 yards away. There it spun back down the slope towards the flag leaving him a ten foot putt to become the

first Briton to don the coveted Green jacket. Sandy's shimmy as his putt slid into the hole for a one-stroke victory over Mark Calcavecchia signalled the start of a new chapter in British golf.

If ever a champion dragged himself off the floor to score a knockout when all seemed lost it was Lyle. He had looked to have squandered his chance by taking a double bogey at the short 12th after going into the water, but a birdie at the 16th put him back on level terms with Calcavecchia, and that was the position when he came to the last hole. The one-iron that Lyle selected in the interests of accuracy and safety, was struck too well, and his ball trickled into the waiting sand. Although the onlookers and millions more on television did not know it, Lyle had no fear of the shot he was then forced to play. 'The ball had rolled slightly up the face of that bunker', he said. 'I knew that if I could pick it off cleanly I would have no trouble getting to the green. The ball was at a perfect angle for take-off and I had been

A shot to be treasured for a lifetime. Lyle chips out from the 18th bunker towards the green 150 yards away. 'I just couldn't bear to look', Lyle's father exclaimed afterwards

The 18th hole at Augusta, known as Holly

practising that shot all week.'

The rest, as they say in the States, is history, but Lyle's victory owed as much to his temperament as his ability to play long bunker recoveries. The Scottish professional's son has an unflappability under pressure that is the envy of all his rivals. He never seems to lose his temper, and that on-course serenity has served him well at moments of crisis before and since . It was first put to the test in the course of winning his first Major title, the Open Championship at Royal St George's, Sandwich in 1985. He had put his second shot at the last into the little hollow left of the final green, and then to everybody's embarrassment, fluffed his little chip to the flag so that the ball ran back down the bank to his feet. To a more volatile personality that incident could have spelt disaster, but Lyle regained his poise, and put his next chip close enough to guarantee a one-stroke win over Payne Stewart. He had the title and was not the least concerned that he had ended on the low note of a bogey. Lyle had won the Tournament Players Championship, the event the Americans like to regard as the fifth Major, the previous year at Sawgrass, beating Jeff Sluman in a nerve-wracking play-off at the third extra hole. In 1988 he had already won twice in the USA, at Phoenix and Greenboro', also after play-offs.

Lyle was therefore in a confident mood when he arrived at Augusta as part of an impressive European contingent which included Ian Woosnam for the first time. Ballesteros, champion in 1980 and 1983 had come a week early to get used to the pace of the greens, and 1985 champion Bernhard Langer was also optimistic . Open champion Nick Faldo and Ken Brown, winner of the Southern Open in Columbus, Georgia following the 1987 Ryder Cup were also there to strengthen the European assault. Although Woosnam was swept to an 81 by the near-gale of the first day, Lyle and Langer both opened with 71 to be only two off the lead. Then the Scot piled in with a 67 to take a two-stroke halfway lead, and kept it with a par 72 in the third. He might have

Sandy is majestically poised on Day 4

done much better for he had two early birdies and with ten holes still to play had spurted to eight under par. Lyle attacked the 13th, looking for a birdie to stretch his lead, but hooked his drive into water and did well to escape with a bogey 6. Then another shot slipped away when he three-putted the 16th, and a six under par total of 210 left the door ajar to too many challengers for comfort. Chief among them was the Texan Ben Crenshaw, winner four years earlier, who moved into a tie for second place with the answer to his putting inconsistency when he played with Nicklaus for two rounds of the Doral Open a month earlier. Lyle explained that he had always felt he was too upright in his putting stroke, and had dropped his right elbow in the manner of Nicklaus, so that it was close to being horizontal to the ground. He found his weight was automatically more evenly distributed, and that he began to swing the putter more with his shoulders than his hands. 'We professionals always look at each

Steering a 15 ft putt towards the hole on the final green — a heart-stopping moment!

Calcavecchia with a 67 in which he birdied the last two holes. Langer, Ballesteros and Tom Watson were also within striking distance when Sandy set out on that last leg on a course that had become increasingly fiery under the effects of wind and hot sunshine. If Lyle had any concern he did not show it. He had coped superbly with the pace of the greens which had so disconcerted Fuzzy Zoeller, despite a second round 66 that he had launched into a public condemnation of the greenkeeper and tournament officials for making the course too difficult. Lyle stayed aloof from the controversy, and in any case he had found other to see if we can learn something that can help us', said Lyle, 'and borrowing from Jack certainly made a big difference to my putting.' During the previous week at Greensboro' Lyle had continually practised his new method, had won the tournament, and was now reaping the benefit at Augusta. A two under outward 34 preserved Lyle's overnight lead, and although Greg Norman was on a typical charge towards a last round 64 he was too far back to concern Lyle.

It was Amen Corner, that stretch of holes around Rae's Creek which have been the scene of so much Masters drama, that almost did for Lyle. Three putts at the 11th

disturbed his equilibrium, then came calamity when he slightly mishit his 8-iron to the short 12th, and it hit the bank of the green and bounced back into the water. He pitched from the dropping area to the rear of the green, and managed to get down in two more for a double bogey 5 — but his lead was gone. Calcavecchia, who was ahead, seized his chance by two-putting for a birdie 4 at the 13th to go into the lead where he was joined by Craig Stadler who had birdied the 14th and 15th to get to six under par. Lyle, having dropped three shots in two holes was now back at five under, and it was very definitely crisis time. Yet, as soon as he surrendered the lead he had held since Friday night, Lyle relaxed. He regained his rhythm almost immediately, although he was unable to get the birdie he needed to draw level, either at the 13th or 15th. When he did draw level it was with a putt of real quality. His 7-iron to the treacherous 16th green had left him some 15 feet above the hole and he simply had to get the pace and line exactly right.

Lyle's ball set off at a snail's pace, then gathered speed and went straight down the steep slope into the middle of the hole. Stadler had set the target with a 68 for a five under 283, but Lyle and Calcavecchia were now both one ahead and each made their par 4 at the 17th. The lack of roars from the 18th green told Lyle all he needed to know when he stepped on to the last tee. 'When my ball dribbled into the sand I thought I was in big trouble', he said. 'The adrenalin was pumping through my body and there was a kind of numbness. When the pressure is on like that the muscles often don't react the way you want them to. It really was a 100 per cent shot.' As every Briton now knows, Lyle was more than equal to the task.

The emotion of the occasion is too much for caddy Dave Musgrove (above left), but Sandy looks well pleased as the Green Jacket fits perfectly

THE OPEN 1990

ST ANDREWS

In front of a record Open audience, Englishman Nick Faldo powers his way to a famous victory.

Faldo examining a difficult looking putt with caddy Fanny Sunesson

They called Nick Faldo the Mechanical Man after he won the 1987 Open Championship by means of a statistically perfect last round of 18 pars. After Faldo won for a second time at St Andrews in 1990, the title of Relentless Robot became a more accurate description. The rest of the world could not match the man who now played golf without malfunction and broke all records for an Open at the home of golf.

Those who had quibbled over his lack of flamboyance at Muirfield, and the element of fortune in his second Masters success via the play-off route that April were made to eat their words. For consistent top quality performance Faldo is now as reliable as the most finely tuned Rolls Royce. All the hours in the workshop of coach David Leadbetter have produced well-oiled golfing machine that is the nearest thing yet to perfection. Faldo has succeeded in eliminating the destructive shot; and when his putting stroke is as smooth as his rhythmic long game, he has no equal.

With a single mindedness not seen in anyone since the early days of Jack Nicklaus, the Englishman has devoted himself to the pursuit of perfection and has now been rewarded with a place in the sporting stratosphere reserved for that elite few who are simply the best. For Faldo work is relaxation, and that is what sets him apart from players who may have greater flair, but are not prepared for one reason or another to commit themselves with the same utmost and thorough dedication.

Before the ll9th Open began Nicklaus had posed the question whether any of the current leading players had the burning desire to reach out for the throne he was reluctantly relinquishing. He wondered who wanted to be that one whom all others wanted to beat, the man whose very presence commanded automatic favouritism. For the best part of 25 years

The massed ranks at St Andrews cheering on their adopted son

Nicklaus had been that eminent being. It was appropriate that he should find his successor that week at sunny St Andrews. It was not one particular round that set Faldo apart from his fellow stars, although the third on the Saturday in company with Greg Norman was the decisive one. It was more his exhibition of unceasing excellence. He began well, consolidated superbly, accelerated beyond reach, and then in true champion's style, dismissed a late challenge to stride home unopposed. Such domination has rarely been achieved by a British golfer, and matched perhaps only by Tony Jacklin in modern times when he won the US Open. Five strokes is an enormous winning margin in such a galaxy of golfing greats, but that was only one of the amazing statistics presented by also fabulous Faldo. His halfway total of 132, also matched by Norman, equalled the previous lowest set by the last Englishman to be a multiple Open champion, the late Sir Henry Cotton, way back in 1934. His 54 hole score of 199 was the first time anyone had ever broken 200, and his 18 under par total of 270 beat the previous St Andrews' best by Seve Ballesteros in 1984 by six strokes.

The four-day attendance record for the Open was also smashed as over 206,000 swarmed into the town, and most of them knew they were on a winner in more ways than one. The punters deprived the bookmakers of more than £1.5 million in successful wagers on Faldo at odds of around 7–1. Robot Faldo was in the right mode from the moment he sank a 45 yards chip and run at the last hole of his first round to open with a 67. The shot was played with a certainty born of supreme confidence as he ran his ball through the Valley of Sin and gently into the hole for an eagle 2 that put him one shot behind the pacemakers Norman and American Michael Allen. The Australian had plundered six birdies from the benign Old Course and for once seemed intent on making a fast start rather than a whirlwind finish. He was responding to the challenge of Faldo to his position as leader of the Sony World rankings which reflect a golfer's form over a three-year period rather than one season. By that yardstick Norman remained the most consistent finisher in the top ten, but Faldo was catching up fast. Five birdies in the first ten holes of Norman's second round, underlined his resolve to regain the title he won in 1986, and then he sank a 70 yards pitch for an eagle at the 14th. That sent the Great White Shark diving to eleven under par, and provoked a predictable response from Faldo and the in-form Ian Woosnam,who had won the two previous European tour events with considerable panache, shooting 60 in Monte Carlo and 62 in the Scottish Open at Gleneagles. The Welshman charged to ten under after 12 holes of the second day, but then fell victim to the Road bunker and three-putted as well to take six. Faldo on the other hand, never looked like making a mistake. He swept out in 32, birdied the 10th as well, then hit a glorious 6-iron off a hanging lie to within a couple of feet of the 15th flag. A seventh birdie at the 16th and a solid par at the Road Hole saw him hand in a 65 to join Norman in the halfway lead at 12 under. They were four shots clear of the pack headed by American Payne Stewart and Australian Craig Parry. Several more dangerous rivals were victims of the halfway axe which fell at an unprecedented 143. Ballesteros, Watson, course record-holder Curtis Strange, and defending champion Mark Calcavecchia all fell by the wayside as did the venerable Arnold Palmer in his last Open. The stage was set for a Faldo-Norman duel to rival that of Watson and Nicklaus at Turnberry 13 years earlier, but it was over almost as soon as it began as Faldo pitched over the Burn for a first hole birdie and stayed firmly in command for the rest of the day. His rock solid putting contrasted sharply with the Australian's hesitancy on the greens, where he three-putted an astonishing five times in a miserable 76.

Magic! Faldo holes out at the last

Extrovert Norman went into hiding after that lesson from Faldo in which the Australian once again showed his fallibility under pressure. The Englishman gained three shots after getting out in 33, although that was by no means the best on a day of brilliant scoring. Both England's Paul Broadhurst and Australian Ian Baker-Finch shot 29 to the turn, getting round respectively in 63 and 64. A birdie at the 11th put Faldo four ahead, then not for the first time Norman gave credence to those who question the quality of his thought processes in the heat of the action. Faldo, in one of his rare mistakes, pushed his drive into an area of gorse at the short par four 12th and from the tee looked in real trouble. The Australian could not reach the green, but took his driver anyway, and deposited his ball in a fairway bunker. Faldo was fortunate, finding his ball clear of the gorse and had no trouble in securing his par 4. Norman splashed out of the sand to the front edge of the green, and three-putted to fall five behind. Another drive into sand at the 13th gave Faldo a comprehensive Norman conquest, and although he dropped a stroke at the 17th, he moved five clear of all challengers with another stroke of genius at the last. His pitch to the 18th almost spun back into the hole to give Faldo a total of 16 birdies and an eagle in his first 54 holes. Round in 67 and the first man to better 200, it was now a question of who was going to be second. Faldo's campaign plan had put him in almost total command of the situation and he had still not made full use of the key weapon in his armoury. That was a metal 2-wood he had included in his bag because he wanted a club that would enable him to hit low boring shots into the wind. It also served as the ideal club from the tee on those occasions when a driver might get him into trouble. He was in only one bunker all week. Faldo used it eight times in his final round of 71 in which there was only one brief period of alarm. That was when Stewart birdied the 12th to get within two shots. Faldo responded with another superb 6-iron shot to the 15th, and secured a birdie from eight feet to put himself out of reach of all challengers. He came home on a roller-coaster of applause, his Swedish caddy Fanny Sunesson marching proudly at his side. She had played an important part by helping the master golfer read the putting lines, just about the only chink in the Faldo armour. It was a time for sweet satisfaction as Faldo raised his arms aloft in response to the salute of the huge crowd. As he cuddled the claret jug, his caddy, his children, and his wife, he exclaimed, 'I had a dream after the US Open I would win at St Andrews. It's good to have my baby back.' It will take an exceptional golfer to prise it off him, for Faldo is now poised to be as dominant in the 1990s as Nicklaus was in his prime.

'I had a dream after the US Open I would win at St Andrews. It's good to have my baby back'

St Andrews, the home of golf, remains the pinnacle of achievement for each and every golfer around the globe

World Series 1990

Akron, Ohio

The mercurial Olazabal defies the most treacherous course in the USA to register a round of 61.

Striding towards a memorable victory

By the end of 1990, a young man finally stepped out of the shadow of Severiano Ballesteros to emerge as the player most likely to reach the pinnacle of his profession. Jose Maria Olazabal had swopped places with Ballesteros in the World rankings, rising to third behind Norman and Faldo, as Ballesteros went in the opposite direction to seventh. In doing so, the 24-year old from Fuenterrabia in north west Spain acquired more ranking points than anyone else, Norman and Faldo included. He also scored a victory both of them envied. It came in the World Series of Golf at Akron, Ohio, where he defeated a field containing every American tournament winner of the past 12 months by the amazing margin of 12 strokes. Olazabal returned an 18 under par total of 262 and won by the biggest margin since Johnny Miller took the Phoenix Open by 14 shots in 1975. On the way he beat the tournament record set by Lanny Wadkins by five, having led by eight shots going into the last round. All this on a course of 7,150 yards, and rated the toughest in the USA.

The Firestone Country club championship layout is regarded as one of the best examples of the work of leading architect Robert Trent Jones. Lakes, bunkers and trees add to the difficulties of extreme length, and the par is only 70. Three of the short holes measure over 200 yards. On the morning of Thursday August 23rd, Olazabal reduced it to 61 strokes. It could easily have been something in the 50s for the Spaniard included one bogey and missed two putts inside six feet in the last four holes. Don Padgett, Firestone's golf director, described Olazabal's round as one of the greatest he had ever seen. Hale Irwin, newly crowned US Open champion, commented, 'He did the almost impossible. I take my hat off to him.' Olazabal accepted their congratulations and carried on pulling away from the field, adding three rounds of 67 for a runaway first

Chipping out from the rough during the first round

victory in the USA, three months after he had gained his first on British soil in the Benson and Hedges International at Cornwall's St Mellion. Three months later he still had instant recall on every shot and putt he played that day when his driving, iron play, and putting synchronised as never before. 'I had played as well from tee to green, but I had never putted as well as that at the same time', he said. 'It was an uncanny feeling. I could not believe my eyes. I was holing everything, and almost every shot was struck as I envisaged it. I can only think that it came about because I was in a very happy frame of mind. I had been to the International in Denver the previous week where everything was perfect and when I got to Akron it was just as good. When I saw the greens I knew I would like them. It is easier to see their breaks than in Europe and they were in perfect condition.'

Olazabal set out with John Huston whom he had met a few weeks earlier in the Dutch Open. As they chatted on the first tee neither could have had an inkling of what was to transpire in the next hour. At the end of it the Spaniard had played four holes and was already five under par. In one of the most sensational starts to any prestige tournament, Olazabal became the first and only name to appear at the top of the leader boards opening with five successive threes which translated into birdie-eagle-birdie-birdie-par. A 1-iron off the first tee to a narrow fairway was followed by a 7-iron which left him a one yard uphill putt for birdie. The putt was true. The 500 yard second, one of only two par fives, is uphill but within reach of two long straight hits. Olazabal was home with a 3-wood, and holed from 15 feet for his eagle 3. The next two par fours measure 450 and 465 yards, but the Spaniard reduced them to just six strokes, firstly hitting an 8-iron approach to six feet, then a 5-iron right over the flag to leave himself a tricky downhill putt of two and a half feet. He made that, and then a similar one from twice as far after he had charged his first putt at the short fifth. The spell was broken at the sixth, another long par 4, where he hit the target with a 6-iron but two-putted from 15 feet, and then came the bogey that was to cost him the chance of a sub-60 return. Olazabal missed the green at the 225 yards seventh with his 3-iron shot and failed with a five foot putt for his par. However, it was a temporary lapse and a fourth birdie at the downhill eighth where his 8-iron approach put him 12 feet from the flag, sent the Spaniard to the turn in 30. He had used his putter only 13 times. After starting for home with a regulation four, Olazabal embarked on another hot streak. The 11th offers one of the few clear cut birdie opportunities at Firestone, and he took it with a 9-iron pitch from 130 yards that finished just one inch from the hole for the easiest of birdie threes.

The 12th (180 yards) fell to a 6-iron shot to six feet, then with his putter still smoking he attacked the 13th, another par 4 over 460 yards. He drove into the perfect position and a good 6-iron put him 20 feet above the hole. It was a terrifyingly fast putt; but Olazabal made it for his third birdie in a row to swoop eight under par. After laying up short of the bunkers at the 14th with a 1-iron, he was on target with a 7-iron approach that left him some 25 feet from the hole. There was a double break on this putt, but Olazabal read it perfectly and birdie number eight fell comfortably into his bag.

The Spaniard was by now almost as excited as the gallery that had grown rapidly with the news of his exploits. After his fourth birdie in a row dropped at the 14th he pulled his shirt up over his face in mock embarrassment. Huston also wanted to hide. He was suffering with a back injury and had always seemed to be playing two shots to every one of his inspired partner. When Olazabal struck a 2-iron shot to the elevated green at the 230 yards 15th and deposited his ball two and a half feet from the pin, Huston looked bemused. Surely the Spaniard was not going to birdie for the fifth hole in a row. Half an inch and a couple of blades of grass prevented it, Olazabal seeing his ball horseshoe out of the cup after slightly pushing the putt his caddy had regarded as a formality. The 16th measures 625 yards, but is all downhill and a drive and 3-iron

A delighted Olazabal displays the trophy to his fans — and there will surely be many more to come

put him 90 yards from the green. This time he could not hole from eight feet, and a putt of between five and six feet lipped out on the 17th. Neither did the 18th, another daunting par 4 so typical of the course, yield a birdie, for Olazabal did well to two-putt from 30 feet. He had already done enough to shake the world of golf, having got home in 31 to lead by four strokes. There were eight birdies, an eagle, eight pars and a bogey on a card which contained only 27 putts.

Olazabal went further and further away from the select field, and waiting for him when he came off the final green was Wadkins, the man whose tournament record he had obliterated. 'You can see what kind of future this guy is going to have', exclaimed the American, who was still singing the Spaniard's praises when he journeyed to Europe to compete in the Austrian Open later that year. 'I told Jose that it was a great victory and I was very happy for him', added Wadkins. 'Then I told him to get the hell out of America and go home.'

Olazabal went on from his Akron triumph to win in Japan for the second year running to emphasise his standing as one of the very best international golfers, but he remains slightly puzzled by his Akron achievement. 'You never know when something like that might happen,' he said. 'I didn't feel I was doing anything special while the tournament was on. It was only later that it sank in. I enjoyed thinking about that 61 for a long time afterwards and when I recall that 12 shot win I shall always remember those four days when every part of my game was in coordination. My job now is to get that feeling more often, and especially in a Major Championship.'

INDEX

Illustrations are indicated by *italic* type, and major sections with illustrations by **bold** type

ACKNOWLEDGEMENTS

The publishers wish to thank the following for help in providing the illustrations.

Allsport Photographic (UK) 16, 36, 44 (right), 52, 72, 78, 95, 98, 99, 101, 109, 114, 119, 120, 121, 122, 123, 136, 137. Simon Bruty 20, 29, 40, 68, 86, 97, 134, 167; Dave Cannon 8, 12, 14, 15, 19 (above), 24, 25, 26, 27, 28, 30, 32, 33, 34, 35, 43, 44, 45 (left), 46, 48, 50, 51, 53, 55, 56, 58, 59, 61, 66, 70, 74, 77, 79, 80, 88 (left), 90, 91, 92, 93, 94, 96, 103, 104, 129, 133 (right), 135, 139, 140, 142, 143, 149, 152, 153, 154, 155, 157, 158, 160, 162, 163, 164; Bob Martin 42; Steve Munday 23, 37, 39, 166; Steve Powell 60, 76; Pascal Rondeau 64; Dan Smith, 21, 49, 100, 165

Allsport Photographic (USA)
Tony Duffy 54; Stephen Dunn 63, 82, 88 (right); James Meehan 87

Matthew Harris 17, 18, 31, 38, 62, 69, 75, 81, 84, 85, 102, 145, 146, 147, 150, 156, 161, 168, 169, 170, 173

Michael Hobbs 22, 57, 71, 73, 107, 110

Phil Sheldon 124, 125, 126, 127, 128, 130, 132, 133 (left)

Sport and General Press Agency 41, 111, 112, 113, 115, 116, 118

We would also like to offer our special thanks to Tony Graham of Allsport Photographic (UK) for his thorough picture research efforts throughout the duration of this project; Hayters and especially Frank Nicklin for his unstinting efforts; and to Valerie Lewis Chandler for compiling the index to this book.